THE CRIPPEN FILE

THE CRIPPEN FILE

Compiled by
JONATHAN GOODMAN

ALLISON & BUSBY
London · New York

First published 1985 by
Allison & Busby Ltd
6a Noel Street, London W1V 3RB
Distributed in the USA by
Schocken Books Inc
62 Cooper Square, New York, NY 10003

British Library Cataloguing in Publication Data
The Crippen file
   1 Crippen, Hawley Harvey
   2 Crime and criminals — England — London
     — Biography
  I Goodman, Jonathan
   364.1'523'0924   HV6248.C687

   ISBN 0 85031 636 7
   ISBN 0 85031 637 5 Pbk

Cover & book design: John Latimer Smith

Printed and bound in Great Britain by
Richard Clay (The Chaucer Press) Ltd, Bungay,
Suffolk

Editor's Note

Only rarely do the reprints and facsimiles of journal material contained herein consist of the entirety of what was originally printed; the usual reasons for excision are to avoid repetition and to save the reader from being misled or confused. In some cases, I have transposed items appearing on a single page of a journal.

My special thanks go to John Latimer Smith, designer of this book. I am grateful to the following, who have helped in particular ways: Albert Borowitz, Richard Boyd-Carpenter; Nick Charlesworth; David and Deirdre Cohen; Undine Concannon, Archivist of Madame Tussaud's, London; Peter Cotes; Clifford Allan Elmer; Joe Gaute; Mary Groff; Jack Hammond; Professor Ned D. Heindel; James Hodge; John A. Hogan, Organiser of the Edgar Wallace Society; Lorna Poole, Archivist of the John Lewis Partnership, owners of Jones Bros. (Holloway) Department Stores; Roy Rodwell of The Marconi Company; Bob Scoales, Reference Librarian, Ealing Central Library; Juliet Simpkins, Press and Publicity Officer, Madame Tussaud's, London; Bill Waddell, Curator of the Crime Museum, New Scotland Yard; John Westmancoat of The British Library, Newspaper Library; Richard Whittington-Egan; Dr Philip H. A. Willcox; Dr Camille Wolff.

Sources of unattributed material:
Page 8: postcard courtesy of Dr Camille Wolff. 9: Photographs by permission of the Commissioner of the Metropolitan Police. 11: The text at the top, an extract from an essay in the *Cleveland Magazine* of January 1985, is reprinted by permission of the author, Albert Borowitz, who also provided the picture on this page and that on page 56. 12: Munyon illustrations courtesy of Professor Ned D. Heindel. 13: Letter and photograph courtesy of Madame Tussaud's Archives, London; the Aural Remedies cautionary note is from a book in Joe Gaute's collection. 16: Miss Melinda May's recollection is from *Survivors' Tales of Famous Crimes*, edited by Walter Wood, Cassell, London, 1916. 22: The framed text is from *Answers* of 10 September 1910. 24: The large drawing of the Bedford, by Nick Charlesworth, is taken, by permission, from one of a series of postcards published by the Badger Press, West Wilts Trading Estate, Westbury, Wiltshire. 28: Photograph, 30: letter, 31: photographs, courtesy of David and Deirdre Cohen. 41: The text at the top is an extract from *I Caught Crippen* by Ex-Chief Inspector Walter Dew, Blackie, London, 1938. 41: Illustrations by permission of the Commissioner of the Metropolitan Police. 42: The cartoon of Newton, by 'Spy' (Leslie Ward), appeared in *Vanity Fair*; the quotation within the text is from *Crippen: The Mild Murderer* by Tom Cullen, The Bodley Head, 1977. 47: Photograph courtesy of Madame Tussaud's Archives, London. 48 and 74: Seymour Hicks's comments come from his book, *Not Guilty M'Lord* (Cassell, London, 1939), and from an article in the *Sunday Dispatch* of 10 December 1939. 54: Quotation from *Crime and Its Detection* (volume II), edited by W. Teignmouth Shore, Gresham Publishing, London, 1931. 54: Photograph by permission of the Commissioner of the Metropolitan Police. 56: End of Willcox's notes courtesy of Dr Philip H. A. Willcox. 56: Illustration by permission of the Commissioner of the Metropolitan Police. 66: The text is an extract from *Sir Richard Muir: A Memoir of a Public Prosecutor*, written by S. T. Felstead and edited by Lady Muir, The Bodley Head, London, 1927. 68: Drawing from *News of the World* of 23 October 1910. 89: Letters courtesy of Dr Philip H. A. Willcox. 92: Copy of reward cheque by permission of the Commissioner of the Metropolitan Police. 94: Cover of *Crippen Horror* from a copy of the book in Joe Gaute's collection. 96: Poster courtesy of Madame Tussaud's Archives, London.

It is 1910; the summer of that year.

Though Edward VII expired shortly before midnight on Friday, 6 May, we are still Edwardians — no disrespect to the Fifth George, whose coronation we look forward to, albeit as much for its spectacle as for its meaning. Immodest to say this, no doubt, but we stage-manage State Occasions superlatively well. (Was it not inspiredly touching, the sight of the dog-loving dead king's terrier, a tiny beast called Caesar, trotting along behind his master's coffin?) There will be no hitches, no unseemly incidents, when George is crowned next year: everything will be tickety-boo. Lesser nations should — they really should — try to learn from our example. The Americans, for instance: the inauguration of their president — what's his name? . . . Taft? . . . something of the sort — was not considered worthy of a pen-picture, let alone a drawing or a photograph, by most British papers. And the Russians: just think what happened at the coronation of the present czar, Nicholas II — there was such a shemozzle, the result of negligence on the part of civil servants charged with distributing bounties, that 3,000 people were crushed to death. Nothing faintly like that could happen here. Lord forbid.

Only last summer, Louis Blériot made the first crossing of the English Channel in a heavier-than-air machine, flying from Calais to a meadow near Dover in a mere thirty-seven minutes; and now another French aviator, Louis Paulhan, has won the £10,000 prize in the *Daily Mail*'s air-race from London to Manchester. Tragic about Charles Rolls, is it not? Having become the first man to fly from England to France and, without touching down, back again, the renowned partner of Mr Royce has been killed during an aeronautical tournament at Bournemouth; which makes him the first Englishman to have perished in a flying accident.

'Every day, in every way, I'm growing better and better' — that is the autosuggestive-healing slogan coined by the French pharmacist, Émile Coué. *Tono-Bungay* is the title of a recent novel by H.G. Wells: 'very contemporary', according to one reviewer, the tale pokes rather alarming fun at the craze for patent medicines, the ease with which quacks fleece. Subsequently, the industrious Mr Wells has published *The History of Mr Polly*. Among other new novels are Arnold Bennett's *Clayhanger*, the first in a trilogy of tales about life in the Five Towns; *Howards End* by E.M. Forster; *Prester John* by a young Scot called John Buchan. Five years ago, in Brooklyn, a Jewish girl, Fannie Borach, won a talent-contest with her rendition of 'When You Know You're Not Forgotten by the Girl You Can't Forget'; now, having taken the sensible step of gentilizing her name to Fannie Brice, she is earning $75 per week as an attraction of Florenz Ziegfeld's *Follies* in Manhattan. In London, quite different *Follies* are drawing crowds to the Apollo Theatre; other West End successes are *Alias Jimmy Valentine* at the Comedy, John Galsworthy's *Justice* at the Duke of York's, *The Arcadians* at the Shaftesbury, a revival of *The Bad Girl of the Family* at the Aldwych, *The Chocolate Soldier* at the Lyric, *The Naked Truth* at Wyndham's, and *Priscilla Runs Away* at the Haymarket. In Paris, where they seem to enjoy terpsichorean entertainments, there are inaugural productions of two ballets: Waslaw Nijinsky is the Favourite Slave in *Scheherazade*, choreographed by Michel Fokine to music by the late Andrey Rimski-Korsakov (a name that George Robey, 'The Prime Minister of Mirth' — not likely to be confused with the actual premier, the Liberal Mr Asquith, who is specially solemn at present, what with his problems with the Lords and the Irish, to say nothing of certain Irish Lords — insists on pronouncing 'Instantly Corsets-Off'), and Tamara Karsavina is *The Firebird*, dancing to music by Igor Stravinsky in a ballet commissioned by Serge Diaghilev. Ralph Vaughan Williams's *Fantasia on a Theme by Thomas Tallis* has been played publicly — not in a concert-hall but at Gloucester Cathedral. Sheet-music for 'Ah! Sweet Mystery of Life' is selling like hot cakes — but going by what one hears whistled and hummed extemporaneously, the most popular popular songs are 'Meet Me Tonight in Dreamland', 'By the Light of the Silvery Moon', 'Down By the Old Mill Stream', Let Me Call You Sweetheart', and 'I Wonder Who's Kissing Her Now'. The first editions of the *Pathé Gazette* newsreel are being shown in Great Britain and the United States; and so are longer, fictive motion-pictures, including *The Wizard of Oz, The Gibson Goddess, The New Magdalene*, starring Pearl White, and D.W. Griffith's *Ramona*, with Mary Pickford.

Early in July, James L. Jeffries came out of retirement — and went back to it after being soundly thrashed by Jack Johnson, the first black prizefight champion. Reports state that at least three Negroes were mortally injured during race-riots occasioned by the defeat of the Great White Hope. (Needless to say, no such disturbances occurred here. Admittedly, we have hardly any Negroes to disturb or be disturbed *about*.)

Vichyssoise, a cold version of hot *soupe bonne femme*, has appeared on the menu of the newly-opened Ritz-Carlton Hotel, Manhattan. A non-alcoholic beverage called Coca-Cola is being imported into Great Britain from the United States. Gordon Selfridge, an American, has opened a department store near the Marble Arch, and — in advance of others, so it is said — there is now a British Woolworth's emporium, situated in Church Street, Liverpool.

'Father's Day' has been observed by a few, most of whom are members of the Young Men's Christian Association.

The Chinese are abolishing slavery.

An attempt is being made to market a substance referred to as 'instant coffee' — something that, surely, will never catch on, not even among the menial classes.

It is 1910; the summer of that year. To be precise, the morning of Thursday, 14 July:

THE DAILY MAIL, THURSDAY, JULY 14, 1910.

MYSTERY OF LONDON HOUSE.

DISCOVERY IN A CELLAR.

MUSIC-HALL SINGER'S DISAPPEARANCE.

A discovery which was made late last night, after an exhaustive police search, at a large house in Hilldrop-crescent, Kentish Town, N.W., has led to the grave suspicion that a Mrs. Cripen, who was well known in the music-hall profession under the name of Belle Elmore, has been murdered and her body secretly buried.

Mrs. Cripen, a strikingly handsome woman, who was an American by birth, lived at No. 39, Hilldrop-crescent, and up to the time of her disappearance some five months ago was an official of the Music-Hall Artists' Guild.

Late in February last Mrs. Cripen ceased to attend at the office, and on inquiries being made it was stated that she was ill and had gone on the Continent to recuperate. In March an announcement of her death abroad appeared in the theatrical newspapers. Some time later suspicion was aroused, and inquiries by the police at the town named in the death notice showed that no such person had died there.

Last evening the house was searched from top to bottom, and then the basement was dug up. Some feet underground the police diggers found some remains, which were taken to the mortuary for detailed examination.

The husband of Mrs. Cripen was an American doctor, who has been in the occupation of the house from the date of his wife's disappearance until two or three days ago.

The police have circulated the following description of the husband:—

Hawley Harvey Cripen, alias Peter Cripen and Franckell Cripen, American doctor, aged fifty, 5ft. 3in.; complexion fresh; hair light brown, inclined to sandy, scanty; bald on top; rather long moustache; mark on the bridge of the nose; wears false teeth and gold-rimmed spectacles; speaks with slight American accent; wears hat on back of his head; is plausible and quiet-spoken.

KAISERIN AND A ROSE.

(From Our Own Correspondent.)
BERLIN, Wednesday.

While picking roses at the castle of Sonderburg last Saturday the Kaiserin pricked herself so severely that a slight inflammation set in near one of the finger-nails of her right hand. One of the royal physicians, who hurried to Sonderburg from Kiel, pronounced the injury quite harmless, and it has now entirely disappeared.

The Kaiserin and Princess Victoria Luise of Prussia to-day arrived at Wilhelmshoehe, where they will be joined by the Kaiser at the end of the month.

THE ERA.
MARCH 26, 1910.

BIRTHS, MARRIAGES, & DEATHS.

The charge for inserting in "The Era" an announcement of a Birth, a Marriage, or a Death, or an "In Memoriam" notice, not exceeding twenty-four words, is One Shilling and Sixpence.

As a guarantee of good faith, the name and address of the sender must accompany each notice.

BIRTHS.

BERNARD.—On March 22, 1910, at 36, Sternhold-avenue, Streatham Hill, S.W., the wife of Kevan Bernard (Blanche Marion), of a son. Both doing well.

MARRIAGES.

O'BRIEN—SMITH.—At St. Alban's Roman Catholic Church, Pontypool, Pat O'Brien to Miss Gertrude Smith, Rev. Father Quigley officiating.

DEATHS.

ARCHER.—On Thursday, March 17, 1910, at the Royal Infirmary, Liverpool, Marie Pritchard, the beloved wife of Frederick Archer, of "Two Little Vagabonds" Co. "Into Thy Hands, O Lord."

ELMORE.—March 23, in California, U.S.A., Miss Belle Elmore (Mrs. H. H. Crippen).

FOX.—March 4, at Utica, N.Y., Imro Fox, magician, aged 60.

THE NORTH LONDON CRIME.

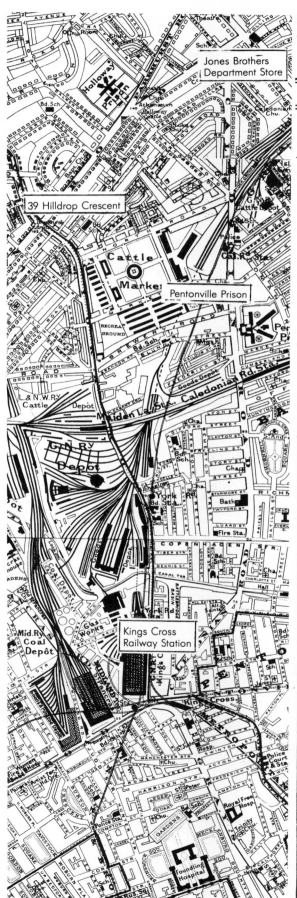

Jones Brothers Department Store

39 Hilldrop Crescent

Cattle Market

Pentonville Prison

Kings Cross Railway Station

Mid.Ry Coal Depot

The New York Times.

NEW YORK, FRIDAY, JULY 15, 1910.—SIXTEEN PAGES.

SEEK CRIPPEN HERE FOR LONDON MURDER

Belle Elmore, Actress Found In a Cellar, Identified as a Brooklyn Woman.

SHIPS TO BE SEARCHED

Discovery of Crime Believed to Have Been Made Through Suspicions of Woman's Friend In New Jersey.

As the result of a request from Scotland Yard the police of this city and Hoboken will to-day begin a systematic search on all arriving steamships which have touched at English ports for Dr. Hawley Harvey Crippen, the American seller of patent medicines, who is wanted on suspicion of having murdered his wife, Belle Elmore, a vaudeville actress, in a house in Hilldrop Crescent, Kentish Town, a suburb of London. Her body was found buried in the cellar of the house.

The immigration officials are also to take part in the search, and yesterday an order was issued by Commissioner of Immigration Williams notifying the members of the boarding division to look out on every vessel for Crippen and the woman who is said to be with him. There is a possibility that the man, if he is headed in this direction, may have had time to catch a steamer at a French port.

According to the belief of the London police, Crippen sailed from England last Saturday. The first of the week-end fleet of steamships to arrive here is the Cunard liner Lusitania, whose arrival was reported last night. She will not come to her pier until this morning. As she anchored off shore all night the police boat Patrol was not sent down to meet her. The police believe there is no chance of the man's escape if he is on board.

Central Office Detectives George Leeson and William Moody will board the vessel from the revenue cutter at Quarantine. They will search for Crippen with the assistance of the immigration officials. When the vessel reaches her pier more detectives and a representative of the British Government will be waiting to reinforce the searchers. The search will be continued upon other arriving vessels until the man is arrested here or the police are satisfied that Crippen and his companion are not bound for America.

Belle Elmore a Brooklyn Woman.

Belle Elmore, the actress, whom Dr. Crippen married, was a Brooklyn woman, and has many relatives in that part of the city, among them her stepfather, Fritz Marsinger, of 685 Grove Street; Mrs. Louise Mills, a stepsister, and the latter's husband, Robert H. Mills; Mrs. Joseph Volkens and Theresa Huhn, other stepsisters, and two stepbrothers, Frederick and Julius Marsinger.

As a child Mrs. Crippen, whose name originally was Cora Kunegunde Makomarsky, was known as Cora Marsinger, having taken her stepfather's name soon after he married her mother.

The last letter written by Belle Elmore to her relatives in this country was received by Mrs. Volkens last Dec. 16. It was dated Dec. 8, and was cheerful in tone. In the letter the actress thanked Mr. and Mrs. Volkens for a photograph of their baby, and expressed a wish that she could have them with her. Her house in London, she said, was too large for herself and her husband, and although they had many acquaintances there none could mean as much to her as her own people. She asked her sister to try to pay her a visit.

Mrs. Mills, who had been at Newport with her husband for several weeks, came to New York yesterday morning upon reading of her stepsister's death.

It was said by the police yesterday that Mme. Ginnett, a trainer of performing horses, who has a farm near Roselle, N. J., was the person who first suspected that there had been foul play. Mme. Ginnett was a close friend of the dead woman, and it was through her activity that the relatives were located in Brooklyn. For several weeks Mme. Ginnett has been making an investigation on her own acount, and last Monday, after she had become convinced that her friend had been made away with, she went to the Brooklyn Police Headquarters and asked the police to aid her in finding the woman's relatives.

Mrs. Mills, one of the stepsisters, when she read yesterday morning's newspapers hurried to the Detective Bureau in Brooklyn and turned over to the police a letter that she and her husband had recently received from Dr. Crippen.

The postmark of the letter showed that it had been mailed in London on April 11 last. The letter was as follows:

39 Hilldrop Crescent,
N. London, England.

My Dear Louise and Robert:

I hardly know how to write you my dreadful loss. The shock to me has been so dreadful that I am hardly able to control myself. My poor Cora is gone, and to make the shock to me more dreadful I did not even see her at the last. A few weeks ago we had news that an old relative of mine in California was dying, and to secure important property for ourselves it was necessary for one of us to go and put the matter in a lawyer's hands at once. As I was very busy Cora proposed she should go, and as it was necessary for some one to be there at once she should go straight through from here to California without stopping at all and then return by the way of Brooklyn, and she would be able to pay all of you a half visit.

Unfortunately, on the way out my poor Cora caught a severe cold, and not having while traveling chanced to take proper care of herself it settled on her lungs. Later it developed into pleuro pneumonia. She wished not to frighten me, so kept writing me that it was only a slight matter, and next I heard by cable that she was dangerously ill, and two days later, after I cabled to know should I go to her, I had the dreadful news that she had passed away.

Imagine, if you can, the dreadful stock to me, never more to see my Cora alive nor hear her voice again. She is being sent back to me, and I shall soon have what is left of her. Of course, I am giving up the house; in fact, it drives me mad to be in it alone, and will sell out everything in a few days. I do not know what I shall do; probably find some business to take me traveling for a few months until I can recover from the shock a little, but as soon as I have a settled address I will write again to you. As it is so terrible to me to have to write the dreadful news, will you please tell all the others of our loss? With love to all, will write soon again and give you my address, probably next in France. From DOCTOR.

ST. PANCRAS CHRONICLE
July 15, 1910.

CAMDEN TOWN CRIME.

ACTRESS MURDERED.

Mutilated Body Found in a Coal Cellar.

The discovery, on Wednesday evening, of a terrible crime enacted at 39, Hilldrop-crescent, Camden Town, created a sensation throughout the district. The body of a woman was found buried beneath the flagstones in the coal-cellar.

Later in the afternoon, Sir Melville Macnaughten, Assistant Commissioner of police, and Superintendent Froest, paid a visit to the premises. Digging operations were commenced in the garden, but the arduous efforts of the officers was not rewarded. Attention was then turned to the house. The removal of some flagstones in the coal cellar, which is beneath the front door steps, revealed a ghastly spectacle. There were found the mutilated remains of the unfortunate victim, the body having been cut up, and large pieces of flesh were lying about in various directions.

The sight, to quote the words of one of the excavators, was absolutely sickening, and enough to knock over the strongest of men.

The strictest possible vigilance is being kept at the premises by the police, and the authorities are busily engaged in scouring the country to ascertain the whereabouts of the woman's husband.

Quite a gloom has been cast over the neighbourhood, and yesterday (Thursday) the vicinity of the crime was visited by thousands of spectators.

One of the deceased's neighbours, seen by a representative of the "Chronicle," said she was surprised inquiries had not been made earlier so quiet had things appeared at the house.

Her own attention was never particularly attracted to the house, she said, but she had wondered whether Mrs. Crippen had gone away.

A representative of a tradesman in Brecknock-road, interviewed, said he knew Mr. and Mrs. Crippen well by sight.

"Mrs. Crippen seemed a very charming woman," he said, "but as for him, I did not like the looks of him at all. He was very bad-tempered and bad looking and seemed to be a man who did a lot of thinking or had a lot of worry. He came to the shop on several occasions to buy goods, which he nearly always carried away himself. He was very particular in his way and awfully abrupt in his manner."

"Did you see much of the supposed deceased Mrs. Crippen?"

"No, not very much. I don't think she did much shopping herself in the district. She was a very well dressed lady, and appeared to be very quiet."

"Had your suspicions been aroused in any way at all by her disappearance?"

"I cannot say that they have to any great degree. But I have noticed that neither of them have been about here very much lately."

A local milkman, also seen by a representative of this paper, said he had been in the habit of delivering milk at 39, Hilldrop-crescent.

"Have you been doing so lately?"

"Oh, yes, up till Monday last," came the ready reply.

"Whom did you see?"

"I saw a foreign girl. She has been there about a fortnight. She could not speak a word of English."

"Did you notice anything strange about her demeanour?"

"No, I cannot say that I did. I did not think of doing so, really."

"When did you see the lady of the house—I mean the deceased—last?"

"I cannot say for certain. People say she has been missing for about six months, but I don't think it is so long as that since I saw her."

"Did you speak to her?"

"Yes. I said 'good morning' to her. She was standing at the bottom of the stairs."

"Did she appear to look troubled at all?"

"Oh, no. She seemed very pleasant. She was always very nice. She was a beautiful woman and about the last woman I should ever think would be murdered."

"When did you see the man of the house last?"

"I have not seen him for some time. I did not see much of him. But he was nothing so nice as she was. He appeared to be a bad-tempered fellow."

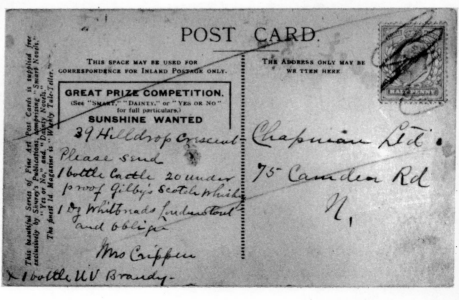

Passage leading to the cellar, showing the excavation.

Grave in the cellar, containing the remains.

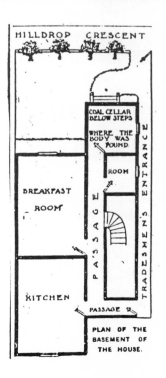

METROPOLITAN POLICE

MURDER

AND MUTILATION.

Portraits, Description and Specimen of Handwriting of HAWLEY HARVEY CRIPPEN, alias Peter Crippen, alias Franckel; and ETHEL CLARA LE NEVE, alias Mrs. Crippen, and Neave.

Wanted for the Murder of CORA CRIPPEN, otherwise Belle Elmore; Kunigunde Mackamotzki; Marsangar and Turner, on, or about, 2nd February last.

Description of Crippen. Age 50, height 5 ft. 3 or 4, complexion fresh, hair light brown, inclined sandy, scanty, bald on top, rather long scanty moustache, somewhat straggly, eyes grey, bridge of nose rather flat, false teeth, medium build, throws his feet outwards when walking. May be clean shaven or wearing a beard and gold rimmed spectacles, and may possibly assume a wig.

Sometimes wears a jacket suit, and at other times frock coat and silk hat. May be dressed in a brown jacket suit, brown hat and stand up collar (size 15).

Somewhat slovenly appearance, wears his hat rather at back of head

Very plausible and quiet spoken, remarkably cool and collected demeanour.

Speaks French and probably German. Carries Firearms.

An American citizen, and by profession a Doctor.

Has lived in New York, Philadelphia, St. Louis, Detroit, Michigan, Coldwater, and other parts of America.

May obtain a position as assistant to a doctor or eye specialist, or may practise as an eye specialist, Dentist, or open a business for the treatment of deafness, advertising freely.

Has represented Manyon's Remedies, in various cities in America.

Description of Le Neve alias Neave.—A shorthand writer and typist, age 27, height 5 ft. 5, complexion pale, hair light brown (may dye same), large grey or blue eyes, good teeth, nice looking, rather long straight nose (good shape), medium build, pleasant, lady-like appearance. Quiet, subdued manner, talks quietly, looks intently when in conversation. A native of London.

Dresses well, but quietly, and may wear a blue serge costume (coat reaching to hips) trimmed heavy braid, about ½ inch wide, round edge, over shoulders and pockets. Three large braid buttons down front, about size of a florin, three small ones on each pocket, two on each cuff, several rows of stitching round bottom of skirt; or a light grey shadow-stripe costume, same style as above, but trimmed grey moire silk instead of braid, and two rows of silk round bottom of skirt; or a white princess robe with gold sequins; or a mole coloured striped costume with black moire silk collar; or a dark vieuxrose cloth costume, trimmed black velvet collar; or a light heliotrope dress.

May have in her possession and endeavour to dispose of same:—a round gold brooch, with points radiating zig-zag from centre, each point about an inch long, diamond in centre, each point set brilliants, the brooch in all being slightly larger than a half-crown; and two single stone diamond rings, and a diamond and sapphire (or ruby) ring, stones rather large.

Absconded 9th inst, and may have left, or will endeavour to leave the country.

Please cause every enquiry at Shipping Offices, Hotels, and other likely places and cause ships to be watched

Information to be given to the Metropolitan Police Office, New Scotland Yard, London S.W., or at any Police Station

E. R. HENRY,
The Commissioner of Police of the Metropolis

Metropolitan Police Office,
New Scotland Yard   16th July 1910

Albert Borowitz writes . . .

Crippen studied first at the University of Michigan, enrolling in 1882 in the School of Homeopathic Medicine. Homeopathy was an alternative school of medicine, then the rage, that favored the administration of minute doses of a remedy that would produce in healthy persons the same symptoms as those of the disease being treated. Crippen did not obtain a medical degree at Michigan but, after a year in London where he pursued his studies, transferred to the Homeopathic Hospital College in Cleveland.

The Cleveland college, founded in 1850, had contributed a bizarre chapter to local history. In 1852, the college building, then on the corner of Prospect and Ontario streets, was attacked and gutted by a mob enraged by the false rumor that a body had been removed from a city cemetery and transported to the school's dissecting room. Undaunted by this disaster, the faculty promptly purchased a large building called The Belvidere on Ohio Street (now Carnegie) near the Haymarket and remodelled it to house the institution.

On Crippen's arrival in Cleveland in 1883, the school stood in its fourth location on Prospect at the corner of Oak Place close to the intersection with Huron Road.

The 1884-85 Annual Announcement of the Hospital College, preserved in the collection of the Howard Dittrick Museum of Historical Medicine at Case Western Reserve University, includes in a list of 1884 graduates the misspelled name of "Crippin, H.H."

The details of Crippen's course of study in Cleveland are unknown. He was later to testify that his curriculum had included a "theoretical" course of surgery.

After his graduation, Dr. Crippen moved to New York and married a student nurse. She bore him a son and in 1892 was close to giving birth to a second child when she died of a stroke. Six months later, at a Brooklyn surgery where he served as assistant physician, Crippen made the fatal acquaintance of 19-year-old Kunigunde Mackamotzki, who had pardonably adopted the simpler name of Cora Turner and was later to call herself Belle Elmore. A large woman with a strong jaw, Belle claimed — without basis — to be the heiress of a Polish nobleman and aspired, despite a weak voice and modest acting ability, to become a star of the musical stage. Crippen was dazzled by her. They married in the fall of 1892.

From the very beginning, things went wrong for the Crippens. A medical problem required the removal of Belle's ovaries, and her plans to prepare for a theatrical career were frustrated by the 1893 depression. Crippen also saw the vogue of homeopathy quickly fade, and he turned instead to the sale of worthless patent medicines for the self-styled Professor Munyon, a huckster.

Prior to 1885, when, at the age of thirty-seven, James Munroe Munyon founded the Munyon Homeopathic Home Remedy Company, with headquarters in Philadelphia, he had been a bobbin boy in a fabric mill, a theatrical agent, and editor or publisher, or both, of journals dedicated to the advancement of workers; between times, he had composed songs. He took free advertising space for his home remedies in *Munyon's Illustrated World*; according to some sources, the money-off coupons that were an invariable component of the advertisements were the first trading stamps. He claimed that his pills and potions were formulated from roots and herbs that he had come across near his birthplace of Thompson, Connecticut; but following the passing of the Pure Food and Drug Act (1906), government analysts found that Munyon's Kidney Cure ('Cures Bright's disease, gravel, all

urinary problems, and pain in the back or groins from kidney diseases') was simply white sugar, that the 'Permanent' Asthma Cure was a mixture of sugar and alcohol, and that the Special Liquid Blood Cure ('Eradicates Syphilis and Scrofula . . . cures enlarged tonsils or glands, ulcers, and all forms of sores and eruptions') was mostly milk-sugar and potassium iodide.

Early in 1894, Munyon engaged Crippen as his New York representative based in an office on East 14th Street, near Sixth Avenue; within a year, Crippen was promoted to the position of general manager of the head offices in Philadelphia; subsequently, he was posted to Toronto to open a Canadian branch. He came to London early in 1897 to open the first overseas subsidiary; his wife followed in the summer.

He returned to Philadelphia in November 1899, and remained there until the first spring of the new century. The duration of the stay seems to contradict the suggestion that Munyon called him back to haul him over the coals concerning the appearance of his name on a programme for a short-lived tour of one-night stands of a show featuring his wife, billed as Cora Motzki, and an apparently Italian tenor called Sandro Vio. (While he was away, his wife enlarged her circle

of men-friends — among whom her special beau was Bruce Miller, a Chicagoan, once a pugilist, who had come to London to perform as a one-man band in music halls.) Crippen's association with the Munyon Homeopathic Home Remedy Company continued for nearly ten years: he was London manager till November 1909, and from then till 31 January 1910 an agent on commission.

He had other sources of income. For instance, starting about 1900, he was 'consulting physician' to a cures-by-post racket that went by the grand-

sounding name of the Drouet Institute for the Deaf. When, following especially bad publicity, the institute foundered, Crippen bought up the assets — including the mailing list, which, in 1906 or thereabouts, became the main foundation of his own Drouetesque firm, the Aural Remedies Company. Two years later, while still both managing Munyon's and dispensing aural remedies, he formed a partnership, as The Yale Tooth Specialists, with an American dentist named Gilbert Rylance.

CONSTIPATION

LIVER   BLOOD

MUNYON'S PAW-PAW PILLS

Dyspepsia   Indigestion

MUNYON'S PILE OINTMENT
For Piles, blind or bleeding, protruding or internal. Stops itching almost immediately, allays inflammation and gives ease to the sore parts. We recommend it for Fissure, Ulcerations, Cracks and such anal troubles.

34   "TRUTH" CAUTIONARY LIST.

was merely a small country doctor, and an " analysis " by a Mr. W. Lascelles Scott (see index). (Vol. 63, p. 1207 ; Vol. 64, p. 1436 ; Vol. 65, p. 820 ; Vol. 66, p. 264.)

116. ARTIFICIAL TEETH AID SOCIETY, LIMITED, 159, New Oxford-street, London, W.C.—A mere advertising shop for the sale of artificial teeth, under the ægis of Lord Haldon. (Vol. 65, p. 11.)

117. AURAL REMEDIES CO., Craven-house, Kingsway, London, W.C.—A firm which runs a treatment ·for deafness on the lines of the late Drouet Institute. It has for " consulting specialist " one H. H. Crippen, M.D., a graduate of an American Homœopathic Hospital College, who was at one time connected with the Drouet Institute, and has also been interested in other quack remedies. (Vol. 66, pp. 1098, 1411.)

An item from *The 'Truth' Cautionary List for 1910*, which gives potted details of persons and organizations investigated by the weekly *Truth* magazine during the preceding two years. Price of the casebound *List*, occupying 128 pages: 1/– net, by post 1/1½d.

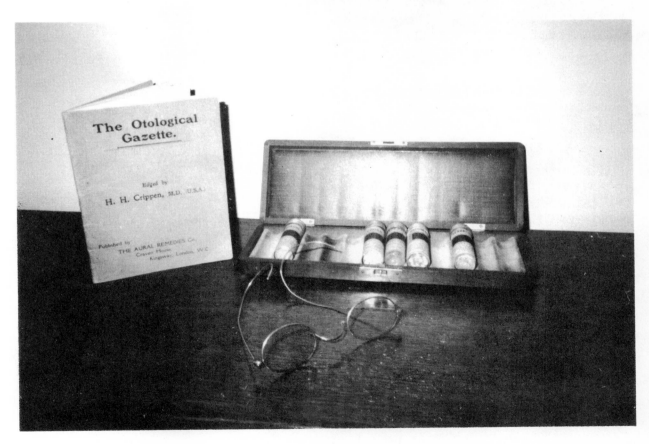

A publication produced by Crippen in aid of his Aural Remedies Coy: his box of Munyon Remedies; and a pair of his spectacles.

HAWLEY HARVEY CRIPPEN.   MISS ETHEL CLARA LE NEVE.

THE DAILY MAIL, FRIDAY, JULY 15, 1910.

THE MYSTERY
OF
HILLDROP-CRESCENT.

WOMAN'S BODY IN A CELLAR.

SEARCH FOR DOCTOR AND TYPIST.

POLICE NARRATIVE.

The mystery of the body found in a cellar at 39, Hilldrop-crescent, Camden Town, on Wednesday, resulted in a notice being issued by Scotland Yard yesterday that Dr. Hawley Harvey Crippen and Miss Le Neve are "wanted for murder and mutilation of a woman."

The following are the dramatis personæ in the mystery:—

H. H. CRIPPEN, American doctor, lived with his wife at 39, Hilldrop-crescent, had offices in Albion House, New Oxford-street, and Craven House, Kingsway; disappeared on Saturday with

MISS LE NEVE, a typist, who had lived at 39, Hilldrop-crescent since February, when

MRS. CORA CRIPPEN, wife of Dr. Crippen, known on the music-hall stage as Belle Elmore, disappeared. The body found in the cellar at Hilldrop-crescent may be hers. Dr. Crippen had inserted in the *Era* a notice of her death in California.

A French girl, who lived at 39, Hilldrop-crescent for the past fortnight apparently as a servant.

ABSCONDING COUPLE.

Yesterday Scotland Yard made a new departure of a most interesting character in their method of crime investigation. The authorities for the first time in their history took the Press into their confidence and issued the following official statement relating to the crime and the steps which led to its discovery:—

Mrs. Cora Crippen, otherwise Belle Elmore, or Belle Mackamotski, an American lady and music-hall artiste, was married some years ago in New York to an American doctor named Hawley Harvey Crippen, alias Peter Crippen, alias Franckel, who for some years represented Munyon's remedies in London, was connected with the Drouet Institute, and has latterly carried on a dental business at Albion House, New Oxford-street, as the Yale Tooth Specialist. Mrs. Crippen was a very charming lady, and was very popular in the music-hall world, and was honorary secretary to the Music-hall Ladies' Guild. They have been in England for some years, and for the past four years they have resided, apparently very happily, at 39, Hilldrop-crescent, Camden-road.

On February 2 last Crippen circulated the report that Mrs. Crippen had left for America to transact business. Later on he said that he had received information from America that she was seriously ill with pneumonia, and later still that she was dead and had been cremated near San Francisco, and that the ashes were on the way to him.

Although her friends were not satisfied with Crippen's story they did not inform the police until June 30 last, when a lady and gentleman friend of hers came to New Scotland Yard and gave information as to her mysterious disappearance to Superintendent Froest and Chief Inspector Dew. Every possible inquiry was made by the latter, who not being satisfied as to Mrs. Crippen's death, interviewed Crippen, who admitted that all his former stories were incorrect and that he had had a quarrel with his wife, who had gone away, saying that she should never see him again, and he believed she had gone to America.

On Saturday last Crippen and Miss Le Neve, whom he had told people he had married, disappeared together about 1 p.m. Chief Inspector Dew, with Sergeant Mitchell, continued the inquiry, made a thorough examination of the house and garden, and on Wednesday afternoon determined to make a still further examination of the garden and the house.

In making a close examination of the cellar, and on probing the brick floor, they found that they could move the bricks in some parts easier than in others, and decided to dig the whole cellar up, with the result that the inspector, after digging some little distance down, came across what was evidently a portion of a human body, and later on the mutilated remains of a body were found.

JULY 16, 1910.

THE ERA.

A VARIETY ARTIST'S FATE.

A ghastly murder, of which a once popular member of the variety profession is believed to be the victim, has been revealed this week. The police have little doubt that some human remains which have been discovered in the coal-cellar of 39, Hilldrop-crescent are those of Miss Belle Elmore, a music-hall artist. Mrs. Cora Crippen, otherwise Belle Elmore, an American lady, was married some years ago in New Jersey to an American doctor named Hawley Harvey Crippen, alias Peter Crippen, alias Franckle, who for some years represented Munyon's Remedies in London, was connected with the Drouet Institute, and has latterly carried on a dental business at Albion House, New Oxford-street, as the Yale Tooth Specialist. Mrs. Crippen was a very charming lady, and was very popular in the music-hall world, and was honorary secretary to the Music Hall Ladies' Guild.

For the past four years they have resided, apparently very happily, at 39, Hilldrop Crescent, Holloway. On Feb. 2 last Crippen circulated a report that Mrs. Crippen had left for America to transact business. Later on he said he had received intelligence from America that she was seriously ill with pneumonia, and later still that she was dead, and had been cremated near San Francisco, and that the ashes were on the way to him.

Although her friends were not satisfied with Crippen's story, they did not inform the police until June 30 last, when a lady and gentleman friend of hers came to New Scotland Yard and gave information as to her mysterious disappearance to Superintendent Froest and Chief-Inspector Dew. Every possible inquiry was made by the latter, who, not being satisfied as to Mrs. Crippen's death, interviewed Crippen, who admitted that all his former stories were incorrect; that he had had a quarrel with his wife, who had gone away, saying that she should never see him again, and he believed she had gone to America.

On Saturday last Crippen and Miss Le Neve, whom he had told people he had married, disappeared together about one p.m. Chief Inspector Dew, with Sergeant Mitchell, continued the inquiry, made a thorough examination of the house and garden, and on Wednesday afternoon determined to make a still further examination of the garden and house.

In making a close examination of the cellar, and probing the brick floor, they found that they could move the bricks in some parts easier than in others, and decided to dig the whole cellar up, with the result that the inspector, after digging some little distance down, came across what was evidently a portion of a human body, and later on the mutilated remains of a body were found. He communicated these facts to New Scotland Yard, when Sir Melville Macnaghten and Superintendent Froest attended and viewed the remains.

Additional details are : that early in February, the following letter from 39, Hilldrop-crescent, but undated, was received by the Committee of the Music Hall Ladies' Guild :

Dear Friends,—Please forgive me a hasty letter and any inconvenience I may cause you, but I have just had news of the illness of a near relative, and at only a few hours' notice I am obliged to go to America.

Under the circumstances, I cannot return for several months, and I therefore beg you to accept this as a formal resigning from this date of the honorary treasurership of the Music Hall Ladies' Guild.

I am enclosing the cheque-book and the deposit-book for the immediate use of my successor, and to save any delay I beg to suggest you should vote to suspend the usual rules of election and elect to-day a new treasurer.

I hope some months later to be with you, and in the meantime wish the guild every success, and I ask my good friends and pals to accept my sincere and loving wishes for their own personal welfare.—Believe me, yours faithfully,
BELLE ELLMORE.

Suspicion was aroused in regard to this letter by the fact that the name "Ellmore" was spelt with two "l's," whereas Mrs. Crippen always signed her name to letters and cheques with one "l." It is believed that the letter was a forgery.

Also, a notice of Mrs. Crippen's death appeared in the obituary columns of *The Era* of March 26 last. It was worded :—

ELMORE.—March 23, in California, U.S.A., Miss Belle Elmore (Mrs. H. H. Crippen).

We were rather inclined to query the notice at the time it was handed in to us, the reason being that we thought we recollected seeing Miss Elmore with some of her friends just a few weeks previously in the office. Still we were not quite sure, but we had the notice endorsed at the back in the usual way by the person handing it in.

Miss Melinda May, the secretary of the Music Hall Artists' Guild, says of Miss Elmore :—"She was a bright, bonny, and beautiful woman, of sweet disposition, and worked very hard for the Guild. We first became suspicious that there was a mystery attached to her supposed departure for California when we received the letter on Feb. 2,

purporting to come from Mrs. Crippen herself, asking me to put someone in her place, because she wished to resign. It was not her handwriting."

Miss May mentioned the strange fact that at the annual dinner of the Music Hall Railway Associations on Feb. 28 Mr. Crippen appeared with his typist, who was very showily dressed. "It was noticed by the majority of our members, who were somewhat startled, that she was wearing a handsome sealskin coat similar to one which had been worn by the deceased, and even then we did not look so much at her fine clothes as at a beautiful brooch she was wearing, which was exactly like a piece of jewellery worn by Mrs. Crippen.

"At the dinner the typist sat at his right hand, and later in the evening Mr. Crippen danced with her. It was given out in some quarters that the typist was his wife."

Mr. Crippen and the late Mrs. Crippen, who is seen seated directly behind her husband.

This photograph was taken in 1909 at the annual dinner of the Music Hall Artists' Railway Association.

Clarkson Rose, actor and music-hall performer, writes:

6 May 1903 was a day to remember, at any rate as far as the Dudley Empire was concerned . . . . It was Dan Leno who stole all the thunder. In fact, the local paper, reporting the show afterwards, only mentioned Dan . . . . On the same programme was Belle Elmore . . . . She wasn't a top-rank artist, but, in her way, not bad – a blowsy, florid type of serio.

I met Dr. Crippen once or twice; he was a quiet, meticulously mannered little man – a great frequenter of the music-halls, and, in fact, attended professionally several variety artists, and somehow I don't think he would have minded the fact that his name was to become a rather macabre music-hall joke, for lots of comedians, in sketches and otherwise, used the slogan, 'Crippen was innocent!' It was a sort of pay-off to an outrageous happening or situation, as, for instance, one well-known comic, discussing in his patter his discomforts as a lodger, ended up by saying, 'Cor blimey! You ought to see the landlady – what a face – Crippen was innocent!'

Miss Melinda May —

I was one of a small party of visitors at Crippen's house on New Year's Eve, 1909. I had been invited to go to see the Old Year out and the New Year in, but I had excused myself on the ground that I was untidy. The doctor and his wife—Belle Elmore—however, must have telephoned to Miss Hawthorne and her husband, Mr. Nash, to call for me, for they came round in Miss Hawthorne's car and took me to 39 Hilldrop Crescent, Holloway. We reached the house at about eleven o'clock, and Miss Elmore went downstairs and made an American cocktail.

At midnight the street door was opened, and there, at the top of the flight of steps which led up to the entrance from the garden path, we stood—the doctor, his wife, Miss Hawthorne and her husband, and myself—to listen to the hooting of sirens, the ringing of church bells, the hammering of trays, and the rest of the strangely moving noises that are made by the watchers who hail the New Year.

Miss Elmore had handed round the cocktail, and we had taken it and had expressed the usual good wishes for the New Year.

" I'm so glad you're here, Miss May," Miss Elmore said, turning to me. " I'm so glad that we're together now, and I do hope that we shall all be together again this time next year."

Poor soul! She uttered those kind and friendly words while she was standing over the very spot where her mutilated remains were buried a month later by the cold-blooded murderer, her husband.

Belle Elmore was at all times kindness and generosity itself; she was a large-hearted woman, and she showed her kindness while we were standing on the top of the steps, for she called up the chauffeur and a constable, who happened to be outside, and invited them to take some refreshment, which they did, joining in the good wishes for the year 1910.

After letting in the New Year we went downstairs to supper; then, at about half-past one in the morning, we left the house, Miss Hawthorne taking me in the car to my residence and afterwards going home.

So the New Year was ushered in, and we settled down to continue and extend our Music Hall Ladies' Guild work, in which Miss Elmore was greatly interested.

The head-quarters of the guild at that time were at Albion House, New Oxford Street, London, where also Crippen had his place of business. The guild has one very special object, and that is to help the poorer women and children of the music-hall profession, so that it is particularly a work for women.

CRIPPEN'S FIRST WIFE.

The Press Association is informed on good authority that the circumstances of the death of the first Mrs. Crippen are now being made the subject of inquiry.

Unfortunately, the formalities necessary have prevented the foreign police from being instantly notified and put on the alert. Astonishing as it may seem, the Paris Criminal Investigation Department yesterday had not been notified that Dr. Crippen and Miss Le Neve were "wanted." The notice has to go first to the Foreign Office, whence it is transmitted to the British Embassy in Paris, when again it is communicated to the French Government, and by them it is forwarded to the French police. This elaborate process gives the offender every chance.

SURPRISE TO THE STEPSON.

Miss Melinda May, honorary treasurer of the Music-hall Ladies' Guild, has found the following letter from the missing man's son by his first wife, Mr. H. O. Crippen, in reply to a letter of inquiry in which Miss May asked for details of the death of Mrs. Crippen, which was stated to have occurred at his house:—

Los Angeles, California, May 9, 1910.

Dear Madam,—I received your letter forwarded to me from the county clerk on April 23, but owing to many misfortunes, sickness, and the death of our son, I overlooked your letter until this date.

The death of my stepmother was as great a surprise to me as to anyone. She died in San Francisco, and the first I heard of it was from my father, who wrote to me immediately afterwards.

He asked me to forward all letters to him and he would make the necessary explanations.

He said he had, through a mistake, given out my name and address as my stepmother's death-place.

I would be glad, if you find out any particulars of her death, if you would let me know of them, as all I know is the fact that she died in San Francisco.—Yours very sincerely,   H. OTTO CRIPPEN.

TYPIST'S "MARRIAGE."
NARRATIVE BY HER FORMER LANDLADY.

An account of the courtship and the supposed marriage between Dr. Crippen and Miss Le Neve was given yesterday by Mrs. Jackson, who in the early part of this year lived in Constantine-road, Hampstead, and with whom Miss Le Neve lodged until she went to live at Hilldrop-crescent.

"The girl, whom I greatly liked," said Mrs. Jackson, "told me that she was very friendly with the doctor and often went out with him. Some time about last August she showed me an engagement ring. She then told me that she was engaged to him.

"Of course, I knew that Dr. Crippen had a wife living, and I asked how she, in those circumstances, could be engaged to him. She replied, 'Mrs. Crippen has been threatening to go away to America with another man. Then the doctor will divorce her—divorce is easy in America—and he is going to marry me.' She said that he was very kind and gentle and always most considerate.

"But a little later I saw that she was unhappy about something, and begged her to confide in me. I told her that she was unwise to be engaged to a man whose wife was alive. She burst into tears and exclaimed, 'Please don't talk to me about it. It makes me so unhappy.' Quite early this year she told me that the doctor had informed her that his wife had gone to America and that he was taking steps to free himself.

"Then one Saturday evening late in January or early in February she came home, bringing Dr. Crippen. They both seemed very happy. Miss Le Neve said, 'See, I have something to show you.' She pulled off her glove and displayed a wedding ring. She said that they had been married that day. She added that they could not go on a honeymoon and they

could not leave the business. That night they went away together to Hilldrop-crescent. Her boxes and other belongings were not taken away for several weeks.

"On two occasions I visited her in her new home. She said she was very happy with her husband and that although they had not had a honeymoon they had spent a few days at Dieppe.

"Miss Le Neve," added Mrs. Jackson, "had a gentle, sweet disposition, and I cannot for a moment believe that she had any part in a crime."

MRS. CRIPPEN'S JEWELS.

Dr. Crippen is stated to have had between £40 and £50 when he absconded. But Mrs. Cora Crippen's jewellery has not been found, and it was valued yesterday by a personal friend at nearly £5,000. She had, it is stated, diamond rings, bracelets, brooches, and affairs.

It is reported that Mrs. Crippen had two private banking accounts, one with the Birkbeck Bank.

The tenant of a house overlooking Hilldrop-crescent informed the London *Evening News* yesterday that six weeks ago she noticed Miss Le Neve in an upper room trying on costumes which she had previously seen on Mrs. Crippen. They were being handed to her by Crippen from a large luggage basket such as is used by theatrical people on tour. He also helped her to fit them on.

The neighbour added that the couple appeared to live almost entirely in the kitchen, the window of which overlooks the back garden. They were seen washing there, they dressed there, and they took their meals there. The blind of this window was never drawn down, and they apparently took no pains to ensure privacy.

"I remember seeing the little French maid playing in the garden with a little brother of Miss Le Neve a week ago last Sunday. I have frequently seen Dr. Crippen helping Miss Le Neve to wash and hang up the clothes—usually on a Sunday."

Miss Le Neve had asked her brother to the house last Saturday, but cancelled the invitation as she had been suddenly "called away."

Miss Le Neve's aunt, Mrs. Benstead, who resides at Hove, stayed with her niece and Dr. Crippen at Hilldrop-crescent last Whitsuntide. She understood that they were married quietly last February at the St. Pancras Registry Office.

With the exception of the French maid, who was brought to Hilldrop-crescent about three weeks ago, the domestic work of the house was carried out by Crippen and his companion, Miss Le Neve, since last February. No charwoman or servant of any kind was engaged to help in the housework. The French girl has been unable to assist the detectives, and has been sent back to her friends in France.

MIDNIGHT SCREAMS.

Mrs. Glackner, of Brecknock-road, whose garden looks on to the back of Hilldrop-crescent, related yesterday that, on a date she could not now fix, but about four or five months ago, she heard screams at midnight.

"Everything round about was quiet, and it seemed to me the screams came from a woman who was horrified at something. I jumped out of bed and pulled up the window, and then I heard another scream, which sounded worse than the first, and I also heard the words: 'Oh, don't! Oh, don't!' coming from No. 39."

STRANGE INFATUATION.

Mr. G. W. Rylance, a New Zealand dentist practising at Albion House, New Oxford-street, informed the *Pall Mall Gazette* yesterday that Crippen was his advertising and business agent.

"A more humble, unassuming little man I have never met, and to me it seems unthinkable that he would have committed so dastardly a crime. I first met him in Munyon's rooms in this building on the occasion of the Kaiser's visit to London. He invited me to look out of his window at the royal procession. For many months afterwards he pestered me to allow him to be my business agent, and eventually I agreed. In my judgment he was a smart man and a wonderful organiser, very exact, with fine business methods; in fact, one could not have desired a straighter representative.

"Of late I had observed that he had looked worried. He had, of course, his bright moments, but generally he appeared to be distressed and perturbed by something or other, and I came to the conclusion that it was due to financial troubles.

"His wife was a woman of charming manners. I frequently saw her here. What passes my understanding is how Crippen could have thrown her over in favour of his typist. It was a strange infatuation. She had little to recommend her as far as I noticed. The typist was a delicate woman. She was always ailing, and was jocularly known in this building as the woman who always answered inquiries with the same remark, 'Not very well, thank you.'"

The *Albion Magazine*, published at 43, Chancery-lane, in an investigation last October of Crippen's "Aural Remedies Co.," of Craven House, reported how the investigator met Crippen in February 1904:

"I remember the man very well indeed, mainly on account of his get-up, and incidentally because of the story to be read in his face. I think Crippen is the only 'physician' I ever met who wore a frock coat together with a remarkably 'loud' fancy shirt, and his 'diamond' stud would have been worth a fortune—if real! His face and eyes told the story of a life miserably misspent. Only a fool would trust Crippen or accept his treatment: his connection with the Drouet Institute speaks for itself."

An American artist's impression of Belle Elmore.

THE NEWS OF THE WORLD

Amazing London Mystery.

WHO BOY-GIRL WAS.

TELLS HER MOTHER SHE WAS CRIPPEN'S WIFE.

However Mrs. Crippen was murdered, and no matter by whom, closely interwoven with her death is the typist's love-story. There can, it seems, be little doubt that Miss Le Neve succeeded to the dead woman's place in Crippen's home. Ethel Le Neve belongs to a respectable family resident in St. Pancras; and, needless to say, her parents are sorely distressed at the notoriety which has overtaken their daughter. The family name is "Neave," not Le Neve. The mother told a press man that she was convinced her daughter had no complicity in the murder, and that she had no idea of going away right up to the day of her disappearance. "My daughter Ethel," said Mrs. Neave, "had been associated with Dr. Crippen in her capacity as shorthand typist for ten or twelve years. One day, a week or two before Easter, she suddenly announced to me, 'I'm married, mother! I've married Dr. Crippen!' I was, you may be sure, more than surprised at the news, for I had not even heard of her engagement. I hastened to question her further. I understood from her that Dr. Crippen had divorced his former wife, and that Ethel and he had been married at a London registry office, which she mentioned. I was more surprised still when she informed me, in answer to my inquiries, that two of Dr. Crippen's friends had acted as witnesses at the marriage ceremony. Dr. Crippen and Ethel spent their honeymoon, which fell at Easter-time, on the Continent, staying most of the time at Dieppe. We received several picture post-cards in pencil from her from Dieppe saying she was well, but no address was given. The pair on their return went to live in Hilldrop-crescent, taking with them a French maid, whom, I believe, they had brought from Boulogne. Since Ethel came back I have told her on four or five occasions when I saw her either here or at her place of business that her father would like

TO LOOK AT HER MARRIAGE LINES,

but she always somehow managed to evade having to produce them. The last time I saw her was on Thursday, July 7, when she came here. On that day she invited Sidney, her little brother, to visit her on July 9, at Hilldrop-crescent, as he had on several occasions since her real or reputed marriage to Dr. Crippen. She also said, 'We are going back to France again soon,' and discussed what arrangements could be made about boarding out the French maid during her absence. Both the fact that she had discussed a trip to France in August and that she had particularly invited Sidney to go to Hilldrop-crescent seem to me to show clearly that she had no idea of disappearing on the day in question. Well, Sidney went to Hilldrop-crescent about 10.45 a.m. At the door of the house the French maid handed a short note in Ethel's writing, which read something like this:—

Very sorry to disappoint you. Called away. Love to all.—Ethel.

That was all. I found afterwards that at about 10.15 a.m. on the morning of her disappearance, Ethel had hurried round in a taxicab to the house of another daughter of mine, and stayed for a few minutes. What her object was I do not yet know." Mrs. Neave added that her missing daughter had lived away from home for nearly a year, during which time the girl had changed her address on several occasions.

Weekly Dispatch

109TH YEAR

THIRD (SATURDAY) EDITION

SUNDAY, JULY 17, 1910.

THE MURDERED WOMAN.

THE WANTED HUSBAND.

Mrs. Crippen, known on the music-hall stage as Belle Elmore.

Dr. Crippen, the missing husband, and a photograph showing the police guarding 39, Hilldrop-crescent, the scene of the murder.

Miss Ethel Clara Le Neve, Dr. Crippen's typist, who is also wanted by the police.

THE DAILY CHRONICLE. MONDAY, JULY 18, 1910.

DR. CRIPPEN MYSTERY.

TYPIST'S STORY OF WHY SHE FLED.

DRAMATIC GOOD-BYE.

A couple of hours before Miss Le Neve vanished with Dr. Crippen on Saturday week, she paid a flying visit to a taxi-cab to her married sister, who lives in a northern suburb of London.

What passed between the two had not been disclosed—even to the police—until last night, when the sister, Mrs. B——, gave an exclusive interview to a representative of "The Daily Chronicle." Her statement gives Miss Le Neve's own story of the circumstances under which she disappeared with the doctor.

The story told by Mrs. B—— to our representative goes clearly to show that her sister could have had no knowledge of Dr. Crippen's grim secret. Mrs. B——'s statement is as follows:—

It must have been, I suppose, about 11 o'clock in the morning when my sister arrived. I was busily engaged with household matters when I heard a knock at the front door. I opened it myself, and, to my great delight, there was Ethel. A taxi-cab was drawn up against the kerb. I had not seen my sister for about a fortnight, and her visit was entirely unexpected.

"Hallo, Ethel," I said. "I am glad to see you."

"Are you alone?" said Ethel. I was surprised at her tone, and I then noticed that she looked a little troubled.

"Yes, I am alone," I said. "Is there anything the matter, darling?"

"Yes, I am afraid there is."

"Oh, come in and tell me all about it. Whatever has happened?"

My sister then followed me into the front room here and tried to explain matters. She seemed excited, and spoke more quickly than usual, frequently repeating herself.

QUESTIONED BY DETECTIVES.

"I am going away," she began. "I had two gentlemen—they were detectives from Scotland Yard—to see me at the house yesterday. They asked me a lot of questions regarding the late Belle Elmore. Her friends are making inquiries. They do not believe she is dead. Therefore, if that is so, I am not Harvey's legal wife."

"After the detectives had questioned me, I went with them in a taxi to the office. There they saw Harvey. What he said to them I don't know, because I was not in the room, and I have not had time to ask him."

"But what is the necessity of going away, dear?" I asked.

"Well," she said, "it is like this. Harvey has an idea of confronting the person who is supposed to have sent the cablegram from California informing him of her death. For all I know she may be alive at this moment. If that is so I cannot be his legal wife."

Ethel is an exceedingly sensitive girl, and I could see that this matter was troubling her a good deal.

"What do you think, dear?" I said.

"Well, of course I don't know," she replied. "For all I know she may be still in London, and have got her friends across

the water to cable to Harvey to inform him of her death. Her idea might be to keep in hiding until we were married, and then to confront him and charge him with bigamy."

She was looking at me rather intently, and I thought she was noticing that my hair was rather untidy.

"Don't look at my hair," I said with a laugh. "I have been busy and have not been able to do it up properly."

"Oh, I am not looking at your hair," was her prompt reply. "Look at mine. I 'scrapped' mine up in a hurry."

I thought she was looking very nice indeed. She was wearing her blue serge costume, and, I think, a large grey hat.

She then took up the thread of her conversation again.

"What is the good of my going with Harvey?" she went on. "Isn't it worrying? But what is the good of my stopping? What good can I be here for the time being? People would look upon me as being no better than a bad woman. It would be no good to stop, so I might just as well go with him."

She then went upstairs to say good-bye to my baby girl, of whom she is very fond. I tried to think of all she had told me, but I could not grasp it then. All that I realised was that she was going away on some strange errand, and this naturally upset me.

"I WILL WRITE YOU."

"Well, good-bye, darling," said Ethel, as I conducted her to the door. "As soon as I know where I am going I will write and let you know."

She then entered the taxi-cab, and smilingly waved a good-bye as she drove away.

When my husband came home I told him that I had had a surprising visit from Ethel, that I gathered there was some talk of Belle Elmore being still alive, and that my sister was going away with the doctor to try to clear up the matter. I heard no more until my husband showed me a newspaper last Thursday reporting the discovery which had been made at Hilldrop-crescent.

You can imagine the shock it gave me. I thought then of all that my sister had told me. She, I am positive, knew absolutely nothing about the murder. She is an exceedingly good girl—a dear sister—and it is impossible to associate her in any way with a crime of any kind.

Indeed, the doctor himself is about the last man in the world whom I would suspect of such an awful deed. I know him very well, and I must say a quieter man I never met. I entered his service at the Drouet Institute ten years ago. I left after about three years to be married, and on my recommendation Ethel, who was then holding a subordinate post in the institute, was appointed in my place. She has been in the doctor's employment at various places ever since.

Some time after the announcement of the death of Belle Elmore my sister told me that she had an "understanding" with the doctor. I was, therefore, not altogether surprised when one Monday morning, early in March, I received this letter from her:—

Darling,—Just a brief note to tell you that we have gone and done it, as the advertisement says. Consequently, I am feeling very happy.

The letter was addressed from Hilldrop-crescent. I imagined at the time that the ceremony had taken place on the Saturday. A little time afterwards the doctor and my sister went to Dieppe for the honeymoon.

When they returned I frequently went to Hilldrop-crescent, and I always found the doctor exceedingly pleasant. He certainly did not seem to have any worry on his mind. A week before Ethel informed me of their marriage the doctor came to our house and stayed about half an hour, but he has not been here since.

Knowing Ethel as I do, I cannot believe that she would stay with the doctor when she learnt the truth! That makes me think that he has taken her out of the country, and carefully kept news of the discovery from her. She is a brave girl, but she would

completely collapse if she heard that the doctor was wanted for murder.

My only fear is that if Dr. Crippen should find himself in a tight corner he may do some harm to my sister. I am waiting anxiously for news that she is safe. It would be a relief to me to know she had been arrested, for I know she could readily clear herself of any complicity in the murder.

LIFE AT THE CRESCENT.

Missing Girl's Friend as Doctor's Guest.

"I have known Ethel all my life," said Miss Lydia Rose, a young lady who had been to school with Miss Le Neve, and had been in close touch with her all through her association with Dr. Crippen:

"Our parents," she said, "were neighbours, and not only did we go to Brock's school together, but she was a constant visitor to my mother's. The intimacy then begun was continued, and when I was living with Lady T——, she used to visit me there, and when I was free we would go out together.

"It was when she lived at Willow-cottages that she went into the City daily to work as a shorthand-typist. It was about five years ago, I should think, that she frequently mentioned Dr. Crippen's name as her employer. When she moved to fresh offices at Albion House, New Oxford-street, I used to go there to meet her. The name on the door was 'Munyon,' but never on any of my visits there did I see the 'doctor.'-Afterwards I remember her telling me that the 'doctor' was working with a Mr. Rylance in a dental business in the same building, and that she had gone there with Dr. Crippen.

"I used to visit her when she lived at Hampstead, and it was just about last Christmas time that she showed me a lovely diamond ring, with four nice-sized stones in it, set on the cross in pairs. She told me then that she was engaged, but she did not say to whom. I did not ask her. I trusted her, and thought that she would have told me if she had wished me to know, and I had such confidence in her.

"QUIETLY MARRIED."

"We saw each other occasionally, and about a fortnight before last Easter—it would be about the beginning of March—I was surprised to receive a letter from her, which read:—

Dear L.,—You will be very surprised to hear your old chum was quietly married last Saturday.

"The letter went on to explain that they could not go away until the Easter vacation, and then they were going to Dieppe. I did not see her before Easter, but on March 25 I received a postcard from Dieppe from Ethel, on which she wrote:—

Darling.—Arrived safely, and had a splendid journey across. Love.—E.

"When she returned," continued Miss Rose, "she wrote to me from Hilldrop-crescent, saying that she was back, and that she wished me to meet her husband; that she hoped we should be good friends, so that we might spend many pleasant evenings together. And we did. I went to Hilldrop-crescent four times, and she introduced me to Dr. Crippen. She told me a relative of the doctor's, who had been living in the house, had gone to America, and that, as he had been staying there, they intended to keep it on.

"I saw the doctor on my first visit. He was most polite and kind in every possible way, and did all he could to make one feel comfortable. He was a very fascinating man, with such a characteristic face that when one had once seen it they would never forget it. His eyes were rather bulging, and he seemed to take in every detail. He would speak in a very quiet way, and when chatting to me told me that he was a little deaf in one ear.

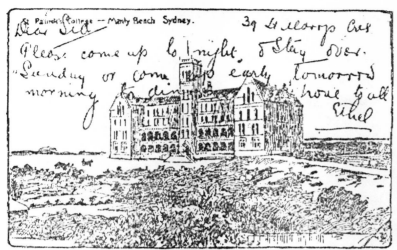

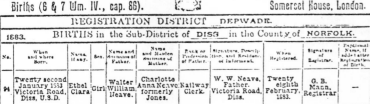

Ethel's picture-postcard inviting her brother Sidney to dinner on the day she disappeared.

"They had no servant then, but when I visited them again, on June 12, Ethel told me she was going to engage a French maid. Then she wrote and told me she had one, and on my next and last visit, on June 26, the French girl was in attendance. They called her 'Valentine.' She could not speak a word of English, and Ethel could not speak much French, and when she spoke to the girl, the doctor, who was a good French scholar, helped her.

A MUSICAL EVENING.

"Ethel was wearing a wedding ring and her engagement ring, but she did not show me much other jewellery. She had some very nice dresses hanging up in her bedroom, and she said they had been made by a dressmaker. When I visited them on June 26 I arrived about 4 o'clock in the afternoon. The doctor opened the door, and showed me into the sitting room. Ethel came from upstairs. We sat chatting about various things until we went downstairs to the morning room in the basement for tea.

"And to think that poor woman was buried so close!" commented Miss Rose with a shudder, " and I was in the house.

"After tea," proceeded Miss Rose, "we returned to the sitting-room and had an enjoyable musical evening, and when I left it was arranged that I should visit them again last Sunday, but I was surprised last Saturday night by the 7 o'clock post to receive a letter from Ethel putting off my visit. I was so disappointed that I tore it up. As far as I can remember it read:—

My dear L,—Do not come up to-morrow. Am not feeling well. Am going away for a few days. Loving wishes, Eth.

"I have heard nothing since. She was, however, such a sweet-tempered, refined girl that I am sure she knew nothing of this terrible affair. She was so kind and of a loving disposition, always ready to give advice when asked. The silly girl, to be led away! I certainly think the wicked man must have some great influence over her which she could not resist. I am certain she had no hand in this crime, because, although not exactly nervous, she was of such a temperament that had she known anything about it she could not have stopped in the house as she did."

Miss Rose added that in the whole of their conversations Ethel, although they were most confidential friends, never mentioned where she was married, or suggested that the doctor had been married previously.

FATHER'S APPEAL.

MR. NEAVE'S LETTER TO HIS DAUGHTER.

Mr. Walter Neave, the father of the missing Miss Le Neve, yesterday handed to a representative of this journal the following open letter to his daughter:—

Sunday, 17.7.'10.

Dear Ethel,—Should this letter by any chance come before your notice, I fervently appeal to you with all a father and mother's love to return to London or give yourself up to the police authorities in whatever country you may be.

Every hour that you stay away you are making the situation terribly worse for yourself. Do wire me instanter.

Assured to you my devotion and protection through this your trouble.

Yours Affectionate
Dad.
Walter Neave

"I am practically certain," said Mr. Neave, "that she is somewhere in France, and it is possible that she will see this appeal from me, her mother, and brothers if *The Daily Mail* will publish it.

"Since they were married both she and Crippen have spent quite a little time in Dieppe, Calais, and other French resorts. They generally stayed in quiet little hotels a little way off the usual track of tourists. Crippen has often told me how fond he is of these secluded retreats, and, excellent French speaker as he is, I am certain that France or Belgium is his hiding place.

"It will not surprise me to hear that he is masquerading as an old woman. His gait, his effeminate mannerisms, and his gentle manner all combine to make such a make-up easy for him. The peculiar marking of his features will, I am sure, impel him to effect some disguise of the sort. His heavy gold-rimmed spectacles will probably have been replaced by goggles."

Certified Copy of an Entry in a Register of Births (6 & 7 Wm. IV., cap. 86).

Given at the General Register Office, Somerset House, London.

REGISTRATION DISTRICT				DEPWADE.					
1883.		BIRTHS in the Sub-District of DISS in the County of NORFOLK.							
No.	When and where Born.	Name, if any.	Sex.	Name and Surname of Father.	Name and Maiden Surname of Mother.	Rank or Profession of Father.	Signature, Description, and Residence of Informant.	When Registered.	Signature of Registrar	Baptismal Name, if added after Registration of Birth.
94	Twenty second January 1883 Victoria Road, Diss, U.S.D.	Ethel Clara	Girl	Walter William Neave.	Charlotte Anna Neave, formerly Jones.	Railway Clerk.	W. W. Neave, Father. Victoria Road, Diss.	Twenty eighth February, 1883.	G. B. Mann, Registrar	—

THE DAILY MAIL, MONDAY, JULY 18, 1910.

THE WANTED DOCTOR AND TYPIST.

Crippen's handwriting
39 Hilldrop Crescent
N.
Feb 4/10

Dear Miss May
Illness of a near relative has called me to America on only a few hours notice, so I must ask you bring my resignation as treasurer before the meeting today so that a new treasurer can be elected at once: You will ...... my haste when I have not been ...... night, packing ... ready to go. I

Le Neve handwriting
39. Hilldrop Crescent

Dear Sir
Am so sorry dear to disappoint you to say have been called away. Will write you later my love, dear. to you all. Kisses
From
your Loving
Ethel

Portraits of Dr. Crippen and Miss Le Neve, with specimens of their handwriting.

ETHEL LE NEVE'S CHARACTER FROM HANDWRITING.

A long letter written by Ethel le Neve, but signed "Ethel," without the surname, was submitted by the Editor of *Answers* to an eminent graphologist, who has furnished the following remarkable delineation of her character from handwriting.   The graphologist had not the faintest clue to the identity of the writer.

"*Ethel*" *is intelligent and rather clever. Impulsive, weak-willed, greatly influenced by those who surround her, and much interested in the opposite sex, she is easily attracted, romantic, morbidly sentimental, and allows her heart to entirely govern her head. At the same time, the handwriting shows distinct traces of selfishness.   Her moods are variable, inclining to melancholy. She is ambitious, and not satisfied with her lot in life. Although "Ethel's" writing is that of a weak-willed person, she is truthful on the whole, and could keep a secret.*

She is careless, but sensitive, and dislikes all coarse or rough things.

Her imagination is inclined to run away with her.

She is extravagant, and not likely to care much for household duties, or to be very wise in money matters.

She strikes me as an easy-going, rather morbid young woman, anxious for masculine admiration —the sort of girl who would make romances out of unromantic things—not strong in any way, but pleasant, generally even-tempered, and loving.

"INTIMATE SOCIETY LETTERS OF THE EIGHTEENTH CENTURY." (See Page 4)

LONDON : TUESDAY, JULY 19, 1910.

No. 6429.—Vol. LXXXIII.   Registered as a Newspaper.

THE CELLAR MYSTERY.

1. MR. LONG, WHO WAS ASKED BY CRIPPEN TO WIND UP HIS HOUSEHOLD AFFAIRS. 2. MR. PAUL MARTINETTI, WHO TOLD OF THE LAST TIME HE SAW MRS. CRIPPEN ALIVE. 3. DR. MARSHALL, WHO MADE THE FIRST EXAMINATION OF THE REMAINS. 4. MRS. MARTINETTI, WHO CORROBORATED HER HUSBAND'S EVIDENCE. 5. MR. WALTER SCHRODER, THE DEPUTY CORONER. 6. CHIEF INSPECTOR WALTER DEW, WHO HAS CHARGE OF THE CASE FOR SCOTLAND YARD. 7. DR. DANFORD THOMAS EXAMINING THE FIRST WITNESS, MR. J. E. NASH, WHO FIRST GAVE THE EVIDENCE TO THE POLICE WHICH LED TO THE DIS-COVERY OF THE CRIME.

SKETCHES AT THE INQUEST AT THE ISLINGTON CORONER'S COURT YESTERDAY.   (See page 7.)

MISS BELLE ELMORE'S DEATH.

Miss Belle Elmore, who is supposed to have been the victim in the Crippen murder case, opened her career at the Old Marylebone Music Hall some twelve years or so ago, where she appeared in a small operetta and wore an embroidered gipsy gown. She appeared at the Grand, Clapham, and the Holborn. She also toured in the provinces. She last appeared at the Bedford Music Hall early in 1907, when she sang a song called " Down Lovers' Walk," and also a coon song. She wore a short spangled dress. She also sang a costume song called " The Major," and appeared in a musical duologue entitled, " The Unknown Quantity." In one of the scenes she had to hold a sheaf of £5 notes. Crippen's desire for realism was so great that he gave her a bundle of genuine bank-notes, which she left on the stage the first night. Fortunately they were seen by her leading man, Mr. Douglas. Others of her songs were, " She never went further than that " and " Sister Mary Ann." In the costume song called " The Major " she appeared in full military costume.

Mr. Harry Goodson, the stage superintendent of the Bedford, says he became acquainted with Belle Elmore about ten years ago. She was at that time a singer whose turn consisted of a tuneful song with a catchy chorus. He wrote two songs for her, which she sang at the Foresters' and the South London. About five or six years ago Belle Elmore left the stage, but, the Bedford being within easy distance of Hilldrop-crescent, she occasionally used to go there with her husband.

Dr. Danford Thomas held an inquest on Monday afternoon, at the Islington Coroner's Court, on the human remains supposed to be those of Mrs. Crippen (Belle Elmore). Several prominent members of the Music Hall Ladies' Guild were present in court, including Mr. H. O. Seyd, the honorary solicitor, Miss Melinda May, honorary secretary, Mrs. Smythson, vice-president, Mrs. Paul Mar-

tinetti, Miss Lil Hawthorne, Mrs. Eugene Stratton, Mrs. C. C. Bartram, Mrs. Gentiro, and Mrs. Fawkes. Chief Inspector Dew, of New Scotland Yard, represented the police authorities.

The main facts of the case are familiar to our readers, and we gladly spare them the evidence relating to the ghastly details of the discovery.

Mr. John Edward Nash, theatrical manager, of Park-mansions, Vauxhall Park, said his wife, Miss Lil Hawthorne, and himself were great friends of Mrs. Crippen, who was the wife of Dr. Crippen, and was theatrically known as Belle Elmore.

The Crippens had dinner at his house on Jan. 19 of this year. That was the last time he saw her alive. On Feb. 2 he heard through his wife that Belle Elmore had resigned from the Music Hall Ladies' Guild. That week Miss Hawthorne was playing at the Tottenham Empire, and he thought it was strange that she should resign so suddenly. My wife, said Mr. Nash, got me to send to her saying we would call on Saturday night, as we wanted to try and talk her into withdrawing her resignation. No one was there; the place was closed, and on Feb. 6 we heard that Belle Elmore had left for California.

From whom did you hear that?—From Miss May, the secretary of the Music Hall Ladies' Guild. It was a big surprise to everyone. On Feb. 27 there was a dinner of the Benevolent Institution, presided over by Mr. Joe Elvin. My wife and I were the guests of Mr. and Mrs. Paul Martinetti. I was very much surprised to see Mr. Crippen enter with his typist. They sat right opposite to us. Mrs. Paul Martinetti recognised that she was wearing one of Mrs. Crippen's brooches, and it made a great impression on me. On March 23 my wife and I sailed for New York. In the first week in May over there we received a letter from Mrs. Paul Martinetti telling us that " poor Belle " had died. About the middle of May we met Mrs. Fred Ginnett, president of the Music Hall Ladies' Guild, in New York, and she was very much upset over Belle Elmore dying. She did not like the look of affairs, so she wrote to the authorities at Los Angeles. She did not get a satisfactory reply.

She got the police of Rochelle, a village where she was staying, to make official inquiries, and then she got a reply to the effect that no such person as Belle Elmore or Mrs. Crippen had died at Los Angeles. Then we felt very bad about it, and thought it was a very mysterious affair. We sailed from New York on June 15. Mrs. Ginnett was there to see us off, and to say "Good-bye," and I promised her that as soon as I arrived in London I would go and interview Mr. Crippen. On June 28 I visited, in company with my wife, Dr. Crippen at his office. That is the first time we had seen him since the reported death of Belle Elmore. We went to offer condolence, and he seemed to be very much cut up. In fact, he sobbed. He seemed to be very nervous, and he was twitching a piece of paper throughout the interview. He gave it out at first that she had died at Los Angeles. When I questioned him he said it was not Los Angeles, but some little town near San Francisco. Not knowing that I had lived for two and a half years in San Francisco, he was rather surprised when I questioned him about a number of the districts. I mentioned several small towns, and he said it was some little Spanish town. I tried to refresh his memory, and I mentioned Alemeda, and he said he thought that was the place. I asked him if he was sure of this, and he said "No," and I said to him, "Peter, do you mean to say that you don't know where your wife has died?" He said he could not remember the place. I then said to him, "I hear you have received her ashes," and he said, "Yes, I have got them in the safe." I asked him the name of the crematorium and about the certificate of death, and he then commenced to get very nervous. He added, "You know there are about four crematoria round there. I think it is one of those." I said, "Surely you have received a certificate?" and he replied, "I think I have got it somewhere."

He was getting very nervous then, and at this time I began to feel that there was something wrong. When a man cannot tell where his wife had died, and whence he has received the ashes of her remains, I make up my mind that there is something wrong, and in this case I determined to communicate with Scotland Yard at once. That was the last occasion I saw him. In company with my wife I went straight to Scotland Yard, and I made an appointment to see Superintendent Froest and Inspector Dew on June 30. I know Superintendent Froest personally. I came over here, and found that no one had had the courage and pluck to take up this matter. I therefore felt it my duty to take action myself.

Mr. H. O. Seyd, solicitor to the Music Hall Ladies' Guild, said he did not know the deceased woman very well, although he had met her on one or two occasions. He added that she fulfilled her duties as hon. treasurer in a very satisfactory way.

Mr. Paul Martinetti said he was a retired music hall artist, and he lived at King Edward's-mansions, Shaftesbury-avenue. He had known Mr. and Mrs. Crippen for about a year. On a certain occasion, said Mr. Martinetti, Crippen called at my flat, and told me his wife had gone to America on very important legal business, and that she might be away for six months. He said something about the possibility of it leading to a title. He also said he should sell his furniture, as he had never liked the house. I called on him next day, and advised him to take the first steamer to America. He did not make any reply to that suggestion, but he said something about his wife having double pneumonia. I offered to assist him in selling his furniture, and in packing his things, but he did not accept the offer, and he never gave me any decisive answers to my questions. I next saw him at the Music Hall Benevolent Fund Ball, with his lady typist. The next time I saw him he called and asked me and my wife to go to dinner with him and the lady typist, and to a theatre afterwards, but we declined the invitation.

Mrs. Clara Martinetti said she became acquainted with Mrs. Crippen about a year and a half ago at "Pony" Moore's house. Belle Elmore persuaded witness to join the Music Hall Ladies' Guild, and they met frequently at Guild functions. On Monday, Jan. 31, she and her husband dined with the Crippens, and left their house about half-past one on Tuesday morning, Feb. 1. That was the last time witness saw Mrs. Crippen alive.

This concluded the evidence taken on Monday, and the inquiry was adjourned till Aug. 15.

THE PERFORMER. July 21, 1910

THE MYSTERY OF BELLE ELMORE.

WHAT THE LADIES' GUILD DID.

It is not necessary for us to devote any considerable amount of our limited space to the sad story of Belle Elmore. Artistes will have followed, with an interest even closer than that of the general public, the column after column in the daily Press slowly unfolding the details of the grim tragedy. It may, perhaps, not be out of place to point out that Miss Elmore's connection with the variety stage as an active professional artiste was a very slight one, but that she was chiefly identified with us (all honour to her memory) through her valuable assistance to the cause of music hall benevolence as hon. treasurer of the Ladies' Guild. This body left no stone unturned in its effort to unravel the mystery of Miss Elmore's disappearance. The facts of the case in this respect are best stated in the words of the following letter to ourselves from Mrs. G. H. Smythson, one of the Guild vice-presidents:—

"Will you please afford me space in your valuable paper to express the feelings of the ladies of the Music Hall Guild, re the words used by Mr. Nash at the coroner's inquest, on Monday, on the remains of Belle Elmore, our lamented hon. treasurer. The words I refer to are these:—'When I found no one had the moral courage and pluck to move in the matter, I went to Scotland Yard.' I now beg to state that on the 31st of March last (one week after poor Belle's death was announced)) I had the 'moral courage' and pluck to go to Scotland Yard, and told them the whole story of the different tales Crippen had given us, also of the incident at the ball with his typist and the brooch she wore. I was under the impression that Scotland Yard kept their eyes on all suspicious persons, but the inspector told me unless I made a definite charge he could not give me any aid. However, the inspector wrote down the names and addresses of several shipping offices and the American Embassy, where I went as soon as I left Scotland Yard. In the meantime, Mrs. Bartram, one of the committee, was in communication with several shipping clerks, re the passenger lists, to find if Miss Elmore's name was there. Miss Davis (Ward and Davis) accompanied me to 39, Hilldrop Crescent, where we knocked and got no reply. Then we went to the neighbours on either side, and inquired if they know when Mrs. Crippen was last seen, and if they saw any luggage go away. Nothing, however, had been seen of her since Monday, January 31st, and no luggage had been seen. Mrs. Martinetti went into Crippen's office with me, when I obtained the address of his son as her deathplace. Mrs. Stratton copied it, and so did Mrs. Martinetti. Then they wrote to Mrs. Ginnett.

"In justice, therefore, to ourselves on the committee, and to our sister members in the country, I contend that the ladies of the Guild did show 'moral courage and pluck,' and if Mr. Nash was fortunate enough to enlist the interest of Scotland Yard four months after my visit, it did not lessen the efforts of the Ladies' Guild, above-mentioned, during his absence in America.

"One of our ladies said yesterday, 'If I had been here, I would have held him; he would not have got away.' But she was told that 'if Inspector Drew could not hold him, you could never have done it.'"

THE TIMES, THURSDAY, JULY 21, 1910.

THE POLICE AND DR. CRIPPEN.

Mr. W. THORNE (West Ham, S., Lab.) asked the Secretary of State for the Home Department whether he could state who was responsible for allowing Dr. Crippen to get out of the hands of the police when it was known by the Chief of the Police at Scotland Yard that Dr. Crippen had made several false statements about the murdered woman which cast suspicion upon the woman's husband that he was responsible for the crime; whether he was aware that the Chief of the Police on June 30 began his investigation on the strength of information given by Mrs. Crippen's friends; whether he was aware that during the investigation the police kept no close watch upon Dr. Crippen, and it was in consequence of the pressing inquiries that caused Dr. Crippen to vanish; and that it was not until July 13 that a search of his house was made, which gave Dr. Crippen three days to get away before the police acted which showed that the Chief of the Police had Dr. Crippen under his observation for nine days and then allowed him to get away; and whether he intended taking any action in the matter.

Mr. MASTERMAN.—If the hon. member will repeat his question later the Secretary of State will endeavour to answer it. It is very undesirable to discuss at the present time details of the important inquiry on which the police are intently engaged.

Mr. W. THORNE.—Can the hon. member suggest when I ought to put the question down again?

Mr. MASTERMAN.—I can only suggest that the hon. member should watch the course of public events.

Mr. W. THORNE.—Or wait until he is captured. (Laughter.)

A favourite recitation at present, this variation on the 'Scarlet Pimpernel' rhyme:

They seek them here, they seek them there,
The bobbies seek them everywhere;
Wondering where have they gone trippin'?—
Ethel Le Neve and Doctor Crippen.

THE SKETCH.

JULY 20, 1910

37

THE MYSTERY OF No. 39—
HILLDROP CRESCENT: WHERE THE CRIPPEN TRAGEDY TOOK PLACE.

THE DAILY TELEGRAPH, MONDAY, JULY 25, 1910.

NORTH LONDON CRIME

WIRELESS MESSAGE
FROM
ATLANTIC LINER.

CRIPPEN BOUND FOR CANADA

WOMAN'S-MALE DISGUISE.

INSPECTOR DEW'S PURSUIT

Scotland Yard authorities are firmly convinced that "Dr." Crippen, who is wanted for the murder which was discovered at 39, Hilldrop-crescent on the 13th inst., and his companion, Miss Ethel Clare Le Neve, are now in mid-Atlantic, bound for Canada.

So certain are the police that their information is correct that on Saturday they despatched Chief Detective-Inspector Dew, who has charge of the case, in pursuit of the fugitives, and it is hoped that he will be able to arrest them on their arrival in Canada.

A statement made yesterday by Scotland Yard was in the following terms:

It is believed that "Dr." Crippen and Miss Le Neve are now on board a vessel bound for Canada.

Chief Detective-Inspector Dew has left Liverpool for Canada, and hopes to overtake the fugitives and arrest them on arrival.

Beyond this the authorities declined to go. We are, however, able to give the full facts of this remarkable discovery and pursuit, of the authenticity of which there is no question.

FLIGHT TO BELGIUM.

"Doctor" Crippen and Miss Le Neve left London on the 9th inst., the day following the first and last interview with Mr. Dew. Undoubtedly the American "doctor" then recognised for certain that the London police were determined to probe to the bottom the mystery of his wife's disappearance. Mrs. Cora Crippen, it will be recalled, was last seen alive by Mr. and Mrs. Martinetti, at 39, Hilldrop-crescent, at 1.30 a.m. on the morning of Feb. 1.

Crippen therefore decided to leave London at once. On Saturday morning, the 9th inst., he sent his employé Long to purchase a boy's suit of clothes and outfit from Messrs. Baker's, in Tottenham-court-road. This was worn by Le Neve. Crippen himself shaved, and leaving behind the suit of clothes he was wearing, put on an attire which might have been that of a street preacher or lay cleric. He also brought about other alterations of his usual appearance, the full details of which are not to hand.

The couple then left for Belgium. Their movements have not been accurately traced, but they are believed to have gone to Brussels, and after that to have spent some days in different quiet country spots in the vicinity. Finding that there was a hue and cry for them in France and Belgium, where it was first suggested in these pages that they had fled, the fugitives apparently determined to attempt an escape to Canada or America.

"MR. ROBINSON AND SON."

It has been ascertained that two persons correctly answering their descriptions, as published by the police, made inquiries in Antwerp concerning outward-bound vessels on July 19. The following day the man, who is now believed by the police to be Crippen, booked a passage for himself and "son" on the Canadian Pacific Company's steamer Montrose, which left London for Montreal on the 14th inst., and arrived at Antwerp on the following day.

The Montrose is one of the slower vessels plying between Europe and Canada, owned by the company named. She has a speed of twelve knots an hour, and carries a few second-class and third-class passengers in addition to cargo. Her masts are fitted with a wireless installation.

The two passengers were booked less than three hours before sailing, second-class, in the name of "Mr. Robinson and son," but they do not appear in the sailing list. The Montrose left Antwerp on the 20th inst. direct for Canada, without any intermediate call. She is due at Montreal on the 30th or 31st. The man, believed to be Crippen, and his companion boarded the vessel hurriedly just before she left the Belgian port. Scotland Yard had detectives looking for Crippen and his typist at Antwerp, but again they managed to escape their vigilance.

THE CAPTAIN'S MESSAGE.

Nothing more was heard of the Montrose until there came a brief but startling message from her captain, that he believed he had the missing doctor and his companion on board his vessel, bound for Canada.

On receipt of this report the whole machinery of Scotland Yard was put into motion, with the object of confirming the particulars. The full official description of the " wanted " couple was telegraphed to the Montrose by wireless. The reply received was a confirmation of the original report, with details of the circumstances which first led the captain to suspect that the " son " in the company of Robinson was a woman.

INSPECTOR DEW IN PURSUIT.

A hurried conference was held at headquarters, and it was decided to send Inspector Dew to Canada by the fast Canadian Pacific liner, the Laurentic, sailing on the following day. Mr. J. Dew joined the vessel at Liverpool on Saturday, and is now well on his way across the Atlantic. A number of reporters and photographers were on the landing stage when the inspector embarked, but he managed to evade them.

The Montrose and the Laurentic are both due on the same day, July 30, but it is hoped and believed that the fast boat will pass the Montrose en route, and arrive a few hours in advance.

Meanwhile the Canadian police have been cabled full instructions to board the Montrose and arrest "Mr. Robinson and son" when the vessel steams into port. It is also hoped that the Laurentic will be able to get into communication with the Montrose on the journey, with the object of advising her captain to keep the suspects under close watch. Owing to the fact that the wireless installation on the Montrose is of a short radius, nothing further has been heard of her, nor is anything likely to be heard until she gets into closer touch with the Canadian shores.

Crippen, it should be added, knows Canada well. For a considerable period he represented Munyon's medicine business at Toronto, and he is believed to have extensively travelled there and in the States.

MONTROSE.

First message, July 22, 1910: Captain Kendall has strong suspicion

THE DAILY MAIL, MONDAY, JULY 25, 1910.

ON THE TRACK OF CRIPPEN

DETECTIVE'S JOURNEY TO QUEBEC.

AN OCEAN RACE.

WIRELESS MESSAGES FROM THE ATLANTIC.

GIRL IN BOY'S DRESS.

For ten days Dr. Crippen and his companion, by twisting and turning on the Continent, avoided detection, but within two days of their breaking into the open and making a dash across the ocean they were recognised. The captain of the Montrose took aboard at Antwerp on Wednesday last, among other passengers, an elderly gentleman and a boy, whose names were given as " Mr. and Master Robinson." By Friday night the suspicions roused almost from the first caused the captain to send a wireless message to this country that he believed he had Dr. Crippen and Miss Le Neve aboard. This was subsequently supplemented by another message to the effect that the person in boy's clothes had been found to be a woman.

There was a hurried consultation at Scotland Yard, where Inspector Dew was engaged till midnight on Friday making preparations to follow and if possible to overtake the Montrose on its way to Quebec. On Saturday he left Liverpool in the fast liner Laurentic, which will be able to pass the Montrose, a comparatively slow boat.

Evidence points to the probability that Crippen was with Miss Le Neve in Brussels on the afternoon of Thursday, July 14. A couple resembling them were seen in a café at a village named Forest, near Brussels. They ordered stout and asked where the " forest " was. This misapprehension could only have arisen where, as in the case of Crippen, there was but an imperfect knowledge of French. M. Loris, the innkeeper, his wife, and several of his guests afterwards recognised the portraits of Crippen and Miss Le Neve which were published in *The Daily Mail*. At this stage Crippen is said to have been clean-shaven, having got rid of his moustache.

For the present there is mystery over the movements of the pair from Thursday, July 14, till Wednesday, July 20. Certain it is that at some time during that period Crippen must have made his arrangements for leaving Europe and booked a passage from Antwerp in the Canadian Pacific cargo and passenger vessel Montrose, bound for Quebec. When the Wednesday came it was an elderly gentleman with a clean-shaven upper lip and a sprouting beard who went aboard the ship with a well-grown lad. They were " Mr. and Master Robinson."

SUSPICION IN THE SHIP.

Almost from the first they seem to have attracted attention. One of the stewards in the ship first called the attention of the captain to the fact that they resembled Dr. Crippen and Miss Le Neve. Neither of the couple gave any other indication than that they were father and son, with nothing to fear, with no reason to refrain from mixing with the other passengers. What were their feelings can only be surmised.

Friday afternoon must have been a dramatic time on board the ship. Ireland was a hundred and fifty miles astern, and Canada lay in front. The captain, becoming convinced of the identity of the pair, realised that it was necessary to take action while he was within " wireless " reach of the shore. He sent a message—reaching Scotland Yard on Friday night—that he believed he had Dr. Crippen and Miss Le Neve on board. From the time

that message was despatched a ceaseless, unobtrusive scrutiny must have been directed towards the couple, for a few hours later another message arrived from the captain to the effect that it was now known with certainty that " Master Robinson " was in reality a woman.

Inspector Dew was at Scotland Yard. He immediately went to Sir Melville Macnaghten, the Assistant Commissioner, and laid the communications before him. It was decided that Inspector Dew should leave at once in pursuit. Telephone messages to the shipping offices secured the detective his berth. He stayed on at Scotland Yard till past midnight making his arrangements, and early on Saturday morning left for Liverpool to join the Laurentic.

The drama is being played out between the two ships on the ocean. While Crippen and Miss Le Neve are striving to avoid notice in the Montrose, the pursuing vessel Laurentic is day by day getting nearer. She passed Torr Head, the nearest Irish point to Scotland, before 5 a.m. yesterday. Wireless messages are being flashed to and fro between the detective and the captain of the ship ahead. The tension in the Montrose must be extreme. How difficult it must be to keep the secret that a couple of passengers are suspect can only be realised by those who have made long voyages. If they are still at liberty life must be a tragic farce. In some mysterious way there may have crept among the passengers an indication that something is wrong. If so Dr. Crippen, bland and keen, will be one of the first to realise that something is amiss. Then he will have to make his decision as to his course of action. Possibly he may decide to await the course of events and take his chance of liberty on landing.

But it is unreasonable to suppose that he will not before long have gauged the fact that the cracking, snapping, in the " wireless " cabin means that messages about him are flying to and fro across the hundreds of miles of sea. All on board will assume that nothing is amiss, and even those who know most will pretend an ignorance of the fact that the air is quivering with wireless messages transmitted, perhaps, by intervening ships. It will be a voyage which no one aboard will be likely to forget. At the end of it, or before, Dr. Crippen will have to face Inspector Dew, to whom three weeks before he so suavely explained his wife's disappearance. Now the inspector carries with him a grim message from the cellar of No. 39, Hilldrop-crescent.

WIRELESS STATIONS ON THE WAY TO QUEBEC.

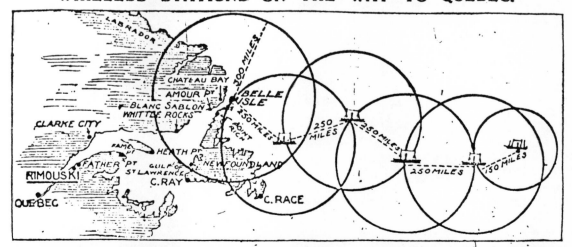

The ships in the above diagram are not the Laurentic and the Montrose, but are meant to illustrate how a vessel of short transmitting power like the Montrose can send a message to another vessel, and that to a third, and so on until it reaches land. The circles indicate the "speaking" radius of each ship. Incidentally it is shown how a ship may speak to the Montrose without the latter being able to answer.

CANADIAN PACIFIC RAILWAY COMPANY.

ATLANTIC STEAMSHIP LINES.

S.S. "MONTROSE,"

July 26th
At Sea   19 10

L. L. Jones Esq.

Marconi Operator

Dear Sir

Please understand that all message re Dr. Crippen to any person or persons on board the above ship, are to be filed, but not delivered, at the same time notifying me of their contents

Yours Faithfully

H G Kendall

(Commander)

This letter from Captain Kendall to Llewellyn Jones, only a few yards away, shows that he is a firm believer in making assurance double-sure.

Captain Kendall

In 1901, he was second officer on the *Lake Champlain*, the first British ocean-going ship to be fitted with Marconi's apparatus. The vessel was off the South of Ireland when the apparatus was shown to be working – by a message from Marconi himself, wishing the master, Captain W. Stewart, successful transmissions and receptions.

THE DAILY MAIL, TUESDAY, JULY 26, 1910.

Carte-de-visite of Llewellyn Jones
Note that Anvers is French for Antwerp.

Llewellyn Jones in the wireless room.

CRIPPEN CHASE.

DETECTIVE IN TOUCH BY WIRELESS.

285 MILES BEHIND.

FUGITIVES' DAYS IN BRUSSELS.

The dramatic chase across the Atlantic of the couple believed to be Dr. Crippen and Miss Le Neve will reach its climax about Sunday.

"Mr. and Master Robinson," described as resembling the fugitives, are on board the Montrose, which left Antwerp for Quebec on Wednesday, July 20; Detective-Inspector Dew is on board the Laurentic, which sailed from Liverpool for Quebec on Saturday last. The Montrose is a comparatively slow boat, the Laurentic is a fast one. The first point of land touched by the ships is 160 miles before Quebec—namely, Rimouski, where incoming ships are boarded by Customs officials. That is where Inspector Dew, having passed the Montrose in the Laurentic, will probably await the arrival of "Mr. and Master Robinson," believed to be Dr. Crippen and his companion. The Laurentic will probably reach Rimouski on Saturday, the Montrose on Sunday.

POSITION OF THE SHIPS TO-DAY

Wireless messages are undoubtedly being transmitted between the Laurentic and the Montrose at the present time. It is possible that by means of intervening ships used as links communications from the Montrose may reach shore in the course of the next day or two. Failing this, it will be the end of the week before a message can be received, the range of the Montrose for transmitting wireless messages being about 250 miles.

At noon to-day the Laurentic will be only 253 knots (about 285 miles) behind the Montrose. The Montrose will approximately be in the position of latitude 53 north and longitude 40 west. The Laurentic should be in latitude 52 north, longitude 33 west. The Laurentic has to make up a leeway of nearly 400 miles in the chase across the Atlantic. A new boat, with a reputation for speed, she ought to be easily able to accomplish the task.

The master of the Montrose, Captain Kendall, is a particularly astute officer of the Canadian-Pacific Line. Quite recently he was chief officer of the Empress of Ireland; promoted to the command of the Milwaukee, he was transferred first to the Monmouth and then to the Montrose. His chief steward, who assisted him and first noticed the suspicious nature of his passengers, is Mr. J. Fawles. Both are highly considered by the company.

POWER OF THE CAPTAIN.

Discussing the position of the captain yesterday an eminent marine lawyer said: "So far as the management of the ship and the safety of the passengers and crew are concerned the captain is absolute master of the situation, and can take any steps which seem, in his judgment, to be necessary. So far as the discipline of the crew and passengers is concerned he can hold any refractory person in custody and hand him over to the judicial authorities upon arriving at a port.

"But in dealing with a case like Crippen's, where a notice has been issued by the police that he is 'wanted,' the captain is in no better or worse position than an ordinary citizen. If the captain is of opinion that the man in his ship is Crippen, he can place him under arrest. If his suspicion is justified, well and good. If, however, the suspect should prove to be someone else, the captain would run the risk of an action at law, claiming damages for false imprisonment. It would then become a question whether the captain had reasonable and probable cause for believing his passenger to be Crippen. If the jury believed that he had, of course no damages would be given.

"In view of the legal position, with which the captain is doubtless well acquainted, it is extremely doubtful whether the man in the Montrose is at present under arrest. It would make no difference to the captain's liability even if the man threatened to put an end to his existence, except that in that event he would render himself liable to the disciplinary laws of the ship."

This is the first instance of the use of wireless telegraphy to identify persons "wanted" by the police.

"There is no doubt," said a senior detective officer yesterday, "that wireless telegraphy is going to play an important part in detective work in the future. It has been used in one or two instances for inquiries on board ships in connection with crimes, but never before have full descriptions of fugitives been sent by wireless telegraphy. It seems that the one thing overlooked by Crippen was the power of communicating between a ship and the outside world."

NINE DAYS IN BRUSSELS.

HOW CRIPPEN SECURED HIS TICKETS.

(From Our Own Correspondent.)

BRUSSELS, Monday.

Inquiries now tend to show that Crippen and Miss Le Neve arrived here on Sunday, the day after the flight from London, and remained in a small hotel for the poorer class until July 18, two days before they embarked at Antwerp. They signed the book as "Mr. Robinson and Son."

I have shown the proprietor and servants of the hotel the enlarged photographs of the fugitives which appeared in the Paris *Daily Mail*, and they at once recognised their strange guests as the wanted couple.

It seems that Crippen first went to the booking-office of the Canadian steamers on July 13, the day that the remains were discovered at his house. He returned to pay the balance of the passage money two days later. Miss Le Neve was with him in boy's dress, but kept out of notice. Crippen insisted on a second-class cabin being reserved for the two.

Although some twenty persons of all nationalities were in the office, the officials think that the photographs I showed them are those of the persons who bought the tickets for the Montrose.

ALERT CANADIAN POLICE.

(From Our Own Correspondent.)

MONTREAL, Monday.

Chief-Inspector Carpenter, of the Montreal detective force, has detailed men to watch the St. Lawrence steamers for suspects. He has given orders for the arrest of Crippen if found.

The Dominion police are also watching the mail station at Rimouski and the Quebec landing-stage.

July 27, 1910   THE DAILY MIRROR

FULL DIARY OF CELLAR CRIME AND HUNT FOR CRIPPEN.

Scotland Yard Issues Official Statement.

PROGRESS OF RACE.

Laurentic with Inspector Dew Overhauling Montrose.

METHOD OF ARREST.

Canadian Policeman to Board the Montrose at Rimouski

TO QUEBEC BY STEAMER.

We publish to-day a complete diary of events in the "Cellar Murder Mystery" case, with the movements of "Dr." Crippen and Miss Le Neve since July 9, when they fled from London.

Scotland Yard has authorised the statement that Chief-Inspector Dew sailed on the Laurentic for Montreal, and that the actual arrest of "Dr." Crippen and Miss Le Neve will be performed by the Canadian police.

Mr. Dew will identify the suspects, says Scotland Yard, and they will be taken into Canadian territory and extradited according to the usual procedure.

No message has been received at Scotland Yard from the Montrose since early on Saturday morning.

The Laurentic is rapidly overhauling the Montrose, and at noon to-day will probably have passed her, taking a much more northerly course, but will certainly be in wireless communication with her.

(Photographs on page 1.)

OFFICIAL STATEMENT.

Scotland Yard officially stated yesterday that Chief-Inspector Dew took the Laurentic for Montreal. The actual arrest of "Dr." Crippen and his companion will be performed by the Canadian police.

Mr. Dew will identify the suspects, who will be taken into Canadian territory and extradited according to the usual procedure.

It is also officially denied that any confession has been reported to Scotland Yard, who have received no message since early Saturday morning.

ARREST TO BE MADE AT RIMOUSKI.

OTTAWA, Tuesday.—Lieutenant-Colonel Sherwood, Superintendent of the Dominion Police, says that no further word has yet been received at Scotland Yard respecting "Dr." Crippen beyond the general instruction issued a fortnight ago asking the police to be on the lookout.

Lieutenant-Colonel Sherwood has instructed Constable Gavreau at Rimouski to board the Montrose on her arrival there to take on board the pilot, and if "Dr." Crippen and Miss Le Neve are on board to effect their arrest and take them to Quebec in the steamer.—Reuter.

DIARY OF CRIME AND HUNT.

The following diary gives a complete summary of all the important events recorded since the crime was first suspected, and it also shows the movements of "Dr." Crippen and Miss Le Neve, from the time they left England up to the time that their presence on board the Montrose was so dramatically disclosed:—

January 31.—Mr. and Mrs. Martinetti dined at Crippen's house, in Hilldrop-crescent, at his invitation. The party played cards. Mrs. Crippen (Belle Elmore) was then in good health.

February 1 (1.30 a.m.).—Mr. and Mrs. Martinetti bade their host and hostess good-bye. That was the last time Mrs. Crippen was seen alive.

February 2.—A forged letter, purporting to come from Belle Elmore, was received by the Music Hall Ladies' Guild, resigning her treasurership on the ground that she had to go to America. Crippen himself confirmed this.

February 27.—Crippen attended the Music Hall Benevolent dinner, accompanied by Miss Le Neve, who wore some of Mrs. Crippen's clothes and jewels.

March 26—Advertisement in English theatrical papers announcing Belle Elmore's death in California.

June 28.—Mr. and Mrs. Nash, who had returned from America, asked Crippen where and when his wife died. Crippen replied evasively, and said her ashes were in his house.

June 30.—Mr. Nash went to Scotland Yard and laid facts before the officials there.

July 8.—Inspector Dew, not finding any trace of the death, interviewed Crippen, who admitted that his previous story about his wife's death was untrue. Said she had quarrelled and had left him.

ARRIVAL IN BRUSSELS.

July 9.—Crippen and Le Neve disappeared from London, and, it is believed, went to Margate.

July 10.—Crippen and Le Neve arrived at a small café in Rue de Brabant, Brussels, and engaged a bedroom. They gave the names of Mr. John Robinson and son. Le Neve was dressed as a boy, and Crippen was not wearing spectacles. It is not known how they got to Brussels, but probably via Dover and Ostend.

July 11.—Police make first discovery of the couple's flight from England.

July 13.—Crippen booked two passages for Quebec, and insisted on having a two-berth cabin.

July 14.—Cellar of Crippen's house in Hilldrop-crescent searched, and the dissected remains of Belle Elmore found buried in quicklime.

July 15.—Police issue photograph of Crippen and full description of him and Le Neve, who they said, "may be dressed as a boy."

BOARDING THE MONTROSE.

July 16.—Photograph of Le Neve, supplied by The Daily Mirror, issued in an amended police notice and sent all over the world.

July 18.—Crippen and Le Neve left the Rue de Brabant, Brussels, and took a room in another part of the town.

July 19.—The hunted couple arrived in Antwerp, and it is supposed slept in a house near the docks.

July 20.—Crippen, who was not in the least disguised, except that he did not wear spectacles and had cut the ends of his moustache, went on board the Montrose with his "son," and eluded detectives who were looking for him.

July 22.—A wireless message from Captain Kendall, of the Montrose, announced to the police that Crippen and Le Neve were suspected to be among the passengers for Quebec.

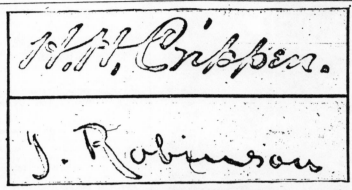

Crippen's ordinary signature and his entry in the visitors' book at the café where he stayed at Brussels. They are enlarged for purposes of comparison. It will be noticed that the "n's" in Crippen and Robinson are very similar. A reference to page one will show that the "e's" in Quebec and Crippen are also much alike.

July 23.—Chief-Inspector Dew dispatched in pursuit on her present voyage," said an expert on the White Star liner Laurentic.

July 24.—Inquiries made by The Daily Mirror in Antwerp fully confirm Captain Kendall's suspicions.

July 25.—Madame Vital, at whose café Crippen and Le Neve stayed in Brussels, gave a full account of their movements to The Daily Mirror, and positively identified their photographs.

PROGRESS OF THE OCEAN RACE.

"The Laurentic is probably being driven at full speed on her present voyage," said an expert navigator to The Daily Mirror yesterday, "and it is not improbable that she may be able to communicate with Belle Isle, north of Newfoundland, as early as Wednesday midnight.

"She has been signalled from Belle Isle on previous voyages late on Wednesday evening, having left Liverpool about the same time on the previous Saturday as she did last Saturday.

"Generally fair weather prevails this week in the North Atlantic, and she might possibly make—for her—a record passage. Sometimes she crosses the Atlantic fast and goes slowly up the St. Lawrence; other times she loses in the ocean part of the journey and makes it up in the river.

"I fully expect she will communicate with Belle Isle on Thursday, and possibly on Wednesday night. In any case she will almost certainly be ahead of the Montrose, and have had communication with her, when she signals Belle Isle.

WIRELESS RANGE.

"At noon to-morrow (Wednesday) the Laurentic will already be nearer Belle Isle than the Montrose, but too far off to communicate direct with the shore."

The Montrose was last signalled 100 miles distant from Brow Head, near Crookhaven, in the south-west of Ireland, at 1.39 p.m. last Friday.

The New York Times

Scotland Yard seems to have secured at last a real clue to the whereabouts of Dr. CRIPPEN. As usual, the "securing" was entirely passive, so far as the police authorities were concerned, and was the result, not of anything they had done, but of the thing they did their stupid best to prevent—the wide publication of every known fact concerning the murder of which Dr. CRIPPEN is suspected. This put numberless people at work as amateur detectives, and though it resulted in almost as many false identifications, none of these did any harm and finally a disguised and therefore presumably fugitive pair have been discovered on shipboard who at least may be the much-wanted doctor and his companion.

Even now the English police cling to their futile policy of concealment, and, by forcing everybody to guess as to what steamer carries the suspects, are creating the possibility of a further evasion. Apparently it is the Canadian Pacific boat Montrose, due at Rimouski next Sunday. At any rate tho wireless instruments are snapping frequent messages about two of her passengers, one of them a woman in man's clothing and the other wearing false eyebrows, and if they are not Dr. CRIPPEN and ETHEL LENEVE, why, who are they? That is the whole of Scotland Yard's case against them, so far as known, and though Miss LENEVE has already committed suicide in a Belgian hotel and Dr. CRIPPEN has been seen on the frontier between France and Spain, they are steaming in almost pathetic helplessness toward the St. Lawrence and capture.

Toward what else remains to be discovered. In Canada there will be no trouble as to extradition, but some is likely to arise in London, since the death of the doctor's wife has not yet been conclusively established, and if the prisoner tells a plausible story about the sorry remnants of somebody found in his cellar there may be difficulty in denying it. However, the law is not quite as solicitous for the safety of murderers in England as it is here, and if the man on the Montrose is really he and he doesn't manage somehow to get ashore on Newfoundland or Cape Breton—it is time for him to begin dreaming of ropes with nooses at the ends of them.

That he is still unconscious of the suspicion he has aroused is hardly possible. "Master Robinson" would know the meaning of the curious glances cast her way by everybody on board the steamer to whom her secret has been revealed, and "Mr. Robinson" is well aware of what can be done by wireless telegraph.

Daily Mirror

WEDNESDAY, JULY 27, 1910.

"DR." CRIPPEN'S REFLECTIONS.

ONLY a Robert Browning, in some imaginative monologue, could do justice to the situation as it must be now, on board the s.s. Montrose: only Robert Browning, with his strange gift for peering into the minds of others and for identifying himself with the feelings of people totally unlike himself, could represent to us what must be the sensations of the hunted Crippen and his companion, caged in the floating trap in mid-ocean. In some such glimpse as that he gives us into the tracked and condemned soul of Count Guido Franceschini in "The Ring and the Book," would the poet show us "clever" "Dr." Crippen meditating upon the attitude of the captain of the Montrose as the vessel nears the harbour.

"Was I so clever, after all," thinks the hunted man, "to run into the open? Is it not the first principle amongst the 'wanted' that they must not get free of cover until the hue and cry for them has died down; and that, above all, they must not land anywhere?

"A harbour is the first place watched. One thirsts, one longs, when something is behind one, to get on to the sea. There's a sense of escape in the very wash of the environing waters! But the clever criminal resists the sea. Mysterious voices nowadays whisper across it; invisible hands stretch out upon it; viewless fingers draw near and clutch and hold there. Better a minor lodging in some big city. For I begin to see that the Captain has an odd look in his face. Was I wise (thinks the "clever" Crippen) to come across the sea?

"The situation, were it only definite, would be endurable. But it is a situation shadowed and uncertain. One knows nothing: one suspects, and is, in turn, suspected. I had never known, until now, that an English captain could wear such an ironical expression, or that people—indifferent people travelling in a ship—could take such an interest in my 'son.' I wish I had not said she was my son. Why didn't we agree to pass, plainly, as man and wife? Why, in Brussels, did we live upon pastry, and behave in an odd, hunted manner? Why take a name like Robinson? Robinson is a name to excite suspicion. If you call yourself Robinson everybody thinks you are not Robinson. A name like McKillycrankyquiller is better. That is the sort of name nobody invents. Why didn't I invent it?"

The Captain is always about. Mr. Robinson is always meeting the Captain; and, each time the Captain meets him, he has something to say, ironical smile on face, about Master Robinson who is "so delicate." The viewless voices whisper on. The situation does not in the least agree with Master Robinson, and Mr. Robinson's nerves are visibly affected. Mr. Robinson puts out his hand for his revolver. It is gone.

Such, we imagine, briefly, is this interesting trip on the Montrose. How will it end? In a day or two we shall know. Meanwhile we leave Mr. Robinson wondering why on earth he hadn't the sense to keep quiet, with Mrs. (not Master) Robinson, in London.   W. M.

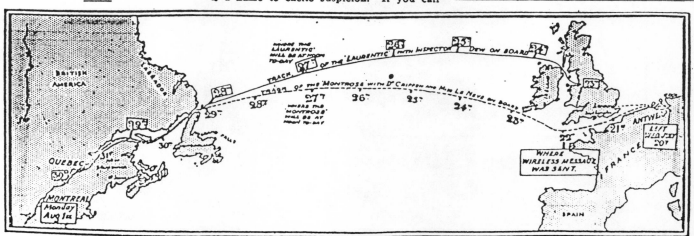

IF ONLY WILLIE CLARKSON HAD HELPED MISS LE NEVE.

THE COMPLETE DISGUISE WHICH ONLY AN EXPERT CAN GIVE.

THE DAILY MAIL, WEDNESDAY, JULY 27, 1910.

CRIPPEN CHASE.

THE 'ROBINSONS' IN BRUSSELS.

(From Our Special Correspondent.)
BRUSSELS, Tuesday.

I have had a long conversation with the landlady of the hotel where "Robinson" (believed to be Crippen) and his so-called son (Miss Le Neve) lived for eight days here after their flight from London. They arrived on Sunday, July 10, three days before the remains supposed to be those of Mrs. Crippen were discovered in the cellar at Hilldrop-crescent, Holloway. On the day of that discovery "Robinson" booked passages in the Montrose for Quebec.

The Hôtel des Ardennes is in the Rue de Brabant, at the back of the Northern Station. There are three storeys, with four tiny rooms on each floor. On the ground floor is a typical Belgian café and restaurant, with a wood and leather bench, the long, numbered clay pipes of the customers, and a show of liquor bottles. The landlady is very stout, with bare arms and a stentorian voice. This is her narrative:

"As the 'father' and 'son' arrived both looked very tired, the 'son' especially. The 'father' was about fifty, small and rather bald. He said, in quite decent French, though with a strong English accent, that he was a merchant from Quebec and had just been travelling on the Continent with his son. He took a room on the first floor at 5s. a day."

Here the landlady took me upstairs. The room is tiny, with a dull yellow wallpaper. The bed takes up nearly all the space. There are a tiny washstand with a broken bit of looking-glass and one chair.

"After two days," the landlady explained, "my husband and I agreed that the boy of sixteen was a girl in disguise. 'He' wore girl's shoes and had a girl's figure."

"Did you not hear her speak?" I asked. "No, she never spoke aloud once all the time we had her here. Her father explained that she was stone deaf, but he was stupid enough to carry on long whispered conversations with her. Now, we always thought deaf people had to be shouted at.

BETRAYED BY HANDS.

"Again, it seemed funny that she always had her hands in her pockets. At last one day they dined here, and we saw that her hands were beautiful and white, with well-kept nails—a woman's hand quite obviously. We never saw her hair, for she always wore a rather large straw hat which concealed it. We called her 'Titine' and nicknamed him 'Old Quebec' because he was always saying, 'My son is ill and must travel. We will go to Rotterdam and thence back to Quebec.'

"We noticed that he read our newspapers eagerly, but he never gave them to his 'son' to read. He always retired to his room when some customer came in, or if he was surprised he spoke to the girl and took her to a dark corner or turned her face so that it was in the shadow. He was usually cool, but appeared unexpectedly at times and rushed to his room. He never left the girl alone one minute. We thought him a professor who had eloped with a girl pupil in disguise.

"After a few days he became more cheerful and even tried to flirt with the maid. On Saturday, July 16, the 'boy' bought some grey canvas shoes and a grey felt hat, which she wore with the rim turned down over the eyes. On Sunday night he said, 'We leave to-morrow. I am very sorry.' He paid for drinks for us all and retired with his silent, pale 'son.' On Monday morning, July 18, after hearty handshakes, the two left with a small valise."

"Did you ever ask about his wife?" I inquired. "Yes; and 'Old Quebec' said, 'Don't speak about that. The poor woman died two months ago in Quebec.'"

"Did he wear spectacles?" I asked. "No, but when he paid the bill he put on a pair to read the figures, but quickly put them back in his pocket."

The landlord struck the table with his fist, and said, "If only we had known it was Crippen! To think I shook hands with him, and then think of the £250 reward! I curse 'Old Quebec'!"

The following is a tracing of "Mr. Robinson's" signature in the visitors' book of the Hôtel des Ardennes, Brussels:—

J Robinson John
Merchant 55 Canada Quebec

I also called at the Red Star Line office, where "Robinson" booked passages for himself and his "son." That these "Robinsons" are Crippen and his typist seems quite clear.

THE CAPTAIN'S MESSAGE.

IDENTITY OF THE COUPLE "FULLY ESTABLISHED."

(From Our Own Correspondent.)
POINT AMOUR (St. Lawrence), Thursday.

Crippen is on board the Montrose, which was 200 miles east of Belle Isle at 12.30 p.m. to-day (Montreal time—i.e., 5.30 p.m. Greenwich).

(From Our Own Correspondent.)
MONTREAL, Thursday Afternoon.

According to a wireless message received from Captain Kendall, of the steamer Montrose at Point Amour station, 600 miles below Quebec, Crippen and Miss Le Neve are aboard.

Their identity has been fully established—"beyond a doubt."

This message was flashed from the Montrose to the Allan liner Grampian, which in turn sent it to Point Amour.

All the wireless stations along the gulf are flashing messages for the Montrose herself, as it is thought that she should be near or coming within her fifty-mile wireless radius of Belle Isle station. That station, which is nearer the open sea than Point Amour, should have picked up the Grampian's relayed message from the Montrose, but it is not working well, and the flash from the Allan liner got by to Point Amour, whence it was first reported.

TIMES OF ARRIVAL.

EAGER CROWD AT FATHER POINT.

(From Our Own Correspondent.)
MONTREAL, Thursday evening.

When the news was flashed from Point Amour that Crippen and Miss Le Neve were really aboard the Montrose, there was the greatest excitement here, in Quebec, and in the summer colony all along the river.

People are now flocking to Father Point in the hope of seeing the arrest. Every farmhouse about Rimouski, every boarding-house, every yacht, sailing and steam, is at a premium.

Sung to the tune of 'Has Anybody Here Seen Kelly?':

Has anybody here seen Crippen,
C R I double-P E N?
Has anybody here seen Crippen? –
Seek him up and down.
He's done a bunk to Can-a-dah
And left his wife in a coal cellar.
Has anybody here seen Crippen,
Crippen from Camden Town?

Sung to the tune of 'Let's All Go Down the Strand':

Crip-*pen* and Miss Le Neve (have a banana) –
England they tried to leave.
Crippen bought a suit of boy's clothes,
Then they went on board the Montrose,
Crippen and Miss Le Neve.

On came Inspector Dew (have a banana);
He said, 'I want you two.
Come back again to England's shore
For the murder of Belle Elmore,
Crippen and Miss Le Neve.'

THE DAILY MAIL, SATURDAY, JULY 30, 1910.

CRIPPEN'S LIFE IN LONDON.

A "DOMESTICATED" HUSBAND.

(By ONE WHO KNEW HIM.)

We have received from Mr. W. Long, who has been associated with Crippen in business for the past twelve years, the following account of the fugitive's life in London:—

I first knew Crippen in 1896 or 1897, when, in answer to an advertisement, I entered his employ. He was then manager to Munyon's remedies in Shaftesbury-avenue. Mrs. Crippen did not come to the business premises for two or three months after I entered the company's service. I saw a good deal of him, of course, and Mrs. Crippen later on used to come to the office of an evening.

They were then living in a flat at Southplace, Tottenham Court-road, and I used to take messages there sometimes. As far as I could see Crippen and his wife were always on the best of terms.

Crippen continued with Munyon's for eighteen months, which were quite an uneventful period. I knew that Mrs. Crippen was on the music-hall stage, and some of her music-hall friends used to come up to Munyon's office.

VISIT TO AMERICA.

Early in 1899 Crippen went to America, Mrs. Crippen remaining behind in London. I saw her several times during this period, but as far as I know she received no letters from him, and I am not aware that she wrote to him. I stayed on in my employment at Munyon's under another manager.

Late in 1899 Crippen returned to London as manager of the Sovereign Remedy Company, off Oxford-street. I heard that he was there, and went to see him, and he took me into his employ again. I was there about a year, and during the whole of that time I never saw Mrs. Crippen there. They were living in a flat in Store-street, Tottenham Court-road.

Crippen left the Sovereign Remedy Company to join the Drouet Institute, and I joined him about three months afterwards as a clerk and head of the shipping department. At first the institute was in Regent's Park-road, but it was afterwards moved to Marble Arch, and here, after a Belgian and a French doctor had left, Crippen took over the whole of the medical business, interviewing the patients, who came to be cured of deafness. Mrs. Crippen never came to the Drouet Institute to my knowledge, but I used to go to the flat in Store-street with messages, and there I sometimes saw Mrs. Crippen.

On the door of the flat in Store-street was written "Belle Elmore, miniature artist." As far as I know she never did any of the painting; but a man who worked with the Sovereign Remedy Company, and another man of the Drouet Institute, used to paint miniatures for Crippen.

At the Sovereign Remedy Company office Crippen also carried on another business which he called "Amorette." It was conducted entirely by Crippen himself and by post. The letters used to come to Store-street, and packets containing the medicine, which was a nerve tonic, were sent out by himself.

Crippen left the Drouet Institute before it closed and rejoined Munyon's, which was then at Oxford-circus. I did not go there

with him for some eighteen months or two years, but during that period I was in frequent communication with him and used to pack tubes of ointment which, under the name of "Ohrsorb," were sold by Crippen as a cure for deafness. I next rejoined Crippen at Munyon's as general assistant, and again Mrs. Crippen did not come to the office.

MOVE TO HILLDROP-CRESCENT.

It is over five years now that the Crippens moved from Store-street to 39, Hilldrop-crescent, Holloway. I helped them to move. They had a lot of very costly furniture. They used to keep a servant then, and she stayed for a few months; but after she left the Crippens were without a servant until Valentine Lecoq, the French maid, came last June. I frequently went to the house with letters, messages, and parcels from Crippen. Mrs. Crippen used to receive them, generally through a little wicket in the side door, and only on two occasions, so far as I remember, did she open the front door. The last occasion was on February 1 (? January 31) this year, when there was a party at the house.

[Mrs. Crippen was last seen alive on the night of January 31-February 1 at a party at which Mr. and Mrs. Paul Martinetti were guests, as they stated at the inquest.]

Crippen, while still at Munyon's, took some offices elsewhere, and carried on his "Ohrsorb" business and also started in the dental business, but he was never a practical dentist and never did any operating, nor did he make false teeth, but employed other people to do this work. He did quite a good business arising from recommendations, but he was not in the offices much himself. He kept the books and attended to the correspondence, but rarely saw any patients.

The first I knew Miss Ethel Le Neve was at the Drouet Institute. She was engaged, not by Crippen, as typist. Her sister had been there before her. I never saw anything other than the ordinary conduct of employer and employed as between her and Crippen. She went to Munyon's when Crippen returned there and to his new offices when he started in the dental business.

Mrs. Crippen used frequently to come to the offices of the dental business during the last year and used to see Miss Le Neve there. Mrs. Crippen used to "pass the time of day" with Miss Le Neve, treating her quite as an employée of Crippen's, neither showing cordiality nor ill-feeling. I did not know that Crippen had any other business while he carried on the dental business.

REMOVAL OF BOXES.

I used to take various parcels and packages from the offices to Hilldrop-crescent, but rarely anything that I could not carry in my hand. On March 2 I went to the offices [Albion House, New Oxford-street] with a carman from Hilldrop-crescent with one tin trunk, a large deal box, locked, but not nailed up, and several cardboard boxes, and also some furniture. When we arrived at the offices before nine in the morning Crippen was there, and several of the packages were taken into the offices by me and the carman.

Others went on in the van—Crippen walked on ahead telling the carman where to take the parcels, but I do not know where they went. I know the carman. A few days later I took more furniture and plants, but no big boxes.

All the packages which were brought from Hilldrop-crescent to Albion House and left there, including the big deal box, have been examined by the police. They are all still there. The big deal box contains silver articles, and the other boxes glass and cutlery.

Crippen never mentioned to me anything about his wife's disappearance. I heard about the end of February that she had gone to California, and Miss Le Neve never mentioned it to me either. I remember the telegram coming that Mrs. Crippen was dead. It was a great blow to me, but I want it to be thoroughly understood that I was never the confidential servant of, or in any way familiar with Crippen.

About the beginning of June I noticed

that Miss Le Neve was wearing a wedding ring. It was after someone had come and asked for Mrs. Crippen, and then Crippen himself said that he and Miss Le Neve had been married.

During all the time I have known him—over twelve years—Crippen has always been a kind and considerate master. He was gentle in his manner, unassuming, never lost his temper, and was a very hard worker. He always appeared on the best of terms with his wife, and was always doing some little service for her, such as sending up a taxicab to the house, buying reels of cotton, matching silk, and would always run to do anything for her.

He never gave me any hint that he was about to leave the country. He was always very reticent about his domestic affairs.

"CRIPPEN SOUVENIRS."

£2 FOR A COLLAR-STUD LEFT IN AN HOTEL.

(From Our Own Correspondent.)

BRUSSELS, Friday.

While the Belgians are interested in Crippen, the English and Americans here are absorbed in the details of the chase. The landlord of the little Hôtel des Ardennes, where Crippen and Miss Le Neve stayed, said to me this evening, "Since you published an account of your visit here in The Daily Mail, English and American people come every day to take photographs and to ask for details of the room which Crippen took.

"Everybody wants souvenirs. A rich Englishman offered me £4 for the page in the hotel book where Crippen wrote his name. But a detective had cut out the page the day after you took a tracing of the signature. An American offered me £2 for a copper collar-stud which Crippen left behind. An Englishman offered me £2 each for two pamphlets left behind by Crippen—one in German, published at Munich, and the other a catalogue of a nursery-gardener at Saffron Walden, in England."

The landlord tells me that Crippen began to look anxious the last few days he was here; evidently this anxiety was caused by news in a Paris Daily Mail, which was afterwards found in his room. Crippen was then spending much less money than previously.

WORLD INTEREST.

EXCITEMENT IN NEW YORK.

(From Our Own Correspondent.)

NEW YORK, Friday.

In momentary expectation of the crucial point of the arrival of the Montrose at Father Point people all over the United States are on the tiptoe of excitement.

To-day all the morning newspapers in New York made the approaching probable capture of Crippen and his companion disguised in boy's clothes the chief feature, some of them illustrating the account with a series of fanciful pictures depicting Crippen's first meeting with Miss Le Neve, the burial of the remains of Mrs. Crippen in the cellar of the London house, the terror-stricken flight of the fugitives, and their apprehensive seclusion in the liner with the wireless operator busy sending and receiving messages to the police authorities.

Early in the day the afternoon newspapers began to issue special editions giving the latest news and surmises regarding the hunted pair. Other editions followed as rapidly as results of the actual wireless communications were received.

PURSUIT BY WIRELESS.

DANGER OF SHIPBOARD FOR FUGITIVES.

LONG ARM OF THE LAW.

Wireless telegraphy is bound to play an important part in the tracking of criminals in the future. Its value has been demonstrated in the past few days. The suspect fugitive flying to another continent no longer finds immunity in mid-ocean. The very air around him may be quivering with accusatory messages which have apparently come up out of the void. The mystery of "wireless," the impossibility of escaping it, the certainty that it will come out to meet a fugitive as well as follow him in pursuit, will from henceforth weigh heavily on the person trying to escape from justice.

"Wireless" makes a ship one of the most dangerous of places for him. If he is known to be on land he may yet find ways of escaping observation and perhaps eventually of getting away altogether. But let a message arrive in a steamer indicating his presence there, and his case is practically hopeless. The captain and his officers have the means of examining for purposes of identity every person in the vessel. An hour or two—or at most a day or two—and the suspect is almost certainly discovered.

If, as is stated in the present case, a captain believes he has fugitives on board, a wireless message sent back to the port he has just left, or sent forward to the port to which he is sailing, means that when the boat reaches land detectives will be in waiting to confront and, if necessary, to arrest the individuals in question. "Wireless" has proved itself of use in procuring help in disaster and now appears likely to prove its value in helping justice. It will be as effective in gripping criminals as it has been in saving threatened men. How it carries the long arm of the law into lonely waters is an interesting process.

THE MAGIC CABIN.

Each ship has on its upper deck a little cabin for the operator, a tiny square erection, wherein two young men take turns by day and night waiting and watching for any word that may come rushing to them from unseen sources behind the horizon. The little cabin, crowded with apparatus, is like a magician's cave. All kinds of appliances are stacked within it. Printed telegraph forms are scattered at one end of the instrument table. The operator on duty is wearing a telephone headgear, with receivers over his ears.

Suddenly there comes to him a low musical note. It is the first indication of a Morse code message. It begins with two or three letters signifying the identity of the ship which is calling. He signals back the letter "K," which means that he is ready to take the communication. As he replies the cabin is transformed. A vivid electric spark throws a weird bluish light over the operator and his machinery. The young man on duty, with a pencil, writes out slowly the message as it arrives. The message may mean suspicion by the authorities of a man aboard the ship. It is hurried to the captain. It may mean that a confederate on shore has transmitted a word of warning to a criminal among the passengers. Again the message is hurried to the captain. In either case the man in question is placed under immediate, though unobtrusive, surveillance. Strict secrecy is observed. None of the passengers know what has been transmitted.

A CHAIN OF MESSAGES.

The difficulty in pursuing criminals by "wireless" is that of getting quick communication between ship and shore. A vessel such as the Montrose throws out her wireless message in a circle all around her 150 miles in every direction. Should a wireless station on land be within 150 miles of her the messages can be transmitted direct. But should the distance be greater, say 500 miles, the Montrose or any similar ship would have to wait till some part of her 150 miles radius, struck that of another ship equipped with a "wireless." This second ship might be nearer land or might be possessed of wireless power with a greater radius, thus enabling her with her higher masts and greater length to out-distance in telegraphing a ship like the Montrose. The Lusitania, for instance, can send messages 300 and sometimes 400 miles. Most of the great liners could keep up direct communication at a distance of 250 miles from the shore station. Ploughing through the sea the ships carry with them a circle of communication, the extent of which varies with their power. It is easily seen therefore that it is far more difficult to get links with a chain of smaller ships than where large ships are available.

Perhaps a steamer like the Montrose with an urgent message to deliver gets in touch with a great liner behind her. The liner flings out the message to the extremity of her power, and it projects far beyond the range of the Montrose ahead. It is taken by another ship, which in its turn sends it forward for other ships to pick up. So it proceeds across the ocean till it reaches land.

But the flying criminal must not think that the ship he is in is prevented from receiving news of him because she happens to have a range of only a few hundreds of miles for sending messages. It is a characteristic of "wireless" that it can be received by ships at a far greater distance than it can be transmitted by them. The result is that steamers a thousand miles from Poldhu are daily receiving messages to which they can make no direct reply to the station on the Cornish coast. Those messages might contain fateful news for a fugitive—though he would know nothing of it till the police came aboard to arrest him at New York.

W. W. BRADFIELD.

A CAGE OF GLASS.

FRENCH POLICE ON THE MARVEL OF WIRELESS.

(From Our Own Correspondent.)

PARIS, Friday.

The French police have been greatly impressed by the invaluable service rendered to Scotland Yard by wireless telegraphy. They recognise that but for its employment the world would still be in ignorance of the whereabouts of the fugitives. The judicial authorities here have now under consideration the extension of wireless facilities as an auxiliary in the capture of criminals at sea.

Commenting on the Hilldrop-crescent tragedy, the *Liberté* says: "Arrest by wireless telegraphy opens a new chapter in criminal history. Thanks to this invisible agent, we are able to follow every movement of Dr. Crippen and his companion. It is admirable and it is terrible. The story of this sensational capture will rank with the greatest wonders of wireless telegraphy. It has served the police well. It has demonstrated that from one side of the Atlantic to the other a criminal lives in a cage of glass, where he is much more exposed to the eyes of the public than if he remained on land."

Master and Mr Robinson on the promenade deck: a clandestine snapping by Captain Kendall, poking his camera through a port-hole.

8   THE DAILY GRAPHIC, SATURDAY, JULY 30, 1910.

THE EXPECTED ARREST OF CRIPPEN TO-DAY OR TO-MORROW.

Map showing the passage of vessels through the Belle Isle Straits.   "Dr." Crippen.

Captain Kendall, of the Montrose.

THE CANADIAN PACIFIC LINER MONTROSE, WHICH IS DUE TO ARRIVE AT FATHER POINT THIS MORNING, HAVING ON BOARD "MR. AND MASTER ROBIN-SON," WHO ARE SUPPOSED TO BE DR. CRIPPEN AND MISS LE NEVE, THE TWO PERSONS "WANTED" IN CONNECTION WITH THE CELLAR MURDER.

THE WESTERN UNION TELEGRAPH COMPANY.

THE LARGEST TELEGRAPHIC SYSTEM IN EXISTENCE.

DIRECT ROUTE FOR ALL PARTS OF THE UNITED STATES.
CANADA, CENTRAL AMERICA, WEST INDIES,
SOUTH AMERICA, & VIA THE PACIFIC CABLE TO AUSTRALIA,
NEW ZEALAND, FANNING, FIJI AND NORFOLK ISLANDS.

ATLANTIC CABLES direct to CANADA and to NEW YORK CITY.
DIRECT WIRES TO ALL THE PRINCIPAL CITIES.

No.

No.	Service Instructions.	Time Received.	WESTERN UNION TELEGRAPH Co. 31 JUL 1910 EFFINGHAM HOUSE, ARUNDEL St, STRAND, W.C.
1288	Col	9.46	
Handed in at		No. of Words.	
Montrose via Father Point que		10	

CABLE OFFICE: EFFINGHAM HOUSE, ARUNDEL St,
STRAND. Telephone 5710 Gerrard.

To   Handcuffs Ldn Eng

Crippen and Leneve
arrested wire later
Dew

The public are requested to hand in their replies at the Company's Stations, where free receipts are given for the amounts charged.
CABLE ADDRESSES ARE REGISTERED FREE OF CHARGE.
No inquiry respecting this Message can be attended to without the production of this Paper.

LLOYD'S WEEKLY NEWS

SPECIAL SUNDAY NIGHT EDITION.

CIRCULATION OVER 1,350,000.

No. 3,532. REGISTERED AT THE G.P.O. AS A NEWSPAPER   LONDON: SUNDAY, JULY 31, 1910. Entered as Second-Class Matter at the New York, N.Y., Post Office, 1903.   ONE PENNY.

FULL STORY OF CRIPPEN'S ARREST.

DISGUISED AS PILOT; INSPECTOR DEW EFFECTS COMPLETE SURPRISE.

"I WANT YOU, CRIPPEN!"

FUGITIVE, RETREATING TO STATEROOM, IS LOCKED UP IN HANDCUFFS.

DECLARES HE IS RELIEVED.

MISS LE NEVE FAINTS ON RECOGNISING THE DETECTIVE.

SAYS SHE IS INNOCENT.

At last "Doctor" Crippen and Miss Le Neve are in the hands of the police.

Their carefully-laid plans of escape have been defeated by means of press publicity and the wireless telegraph.

The first intimation of their arrest was conveyed in the following cable from the Special Correspondent of "Lloyd's News" at Father Point, which reached London at a quarter-past two this afternoon:—

"Father Point, Sunday.—Crippen and Le Neve identified and arrested."

Official intimation of the arrest was received at Scotland Yard from Inspector Dew at 4 p.m.

The inspector was disguised as a pilot, and took his man completely by surprise.

[From "Lloyd's News" Special Correspondent.]

FATHER POINT, QUEBEC,
Sunday, 9.30 a.m. (2.30 p.m. English time).

Crippen and Le Neve have been arrested by the Canadian police on board the Montrose, and are now in their custody.

They were identified by Inspector Dew without any difficulty, and the great ocean race of 3,000 miles has resulted in a victory for Scotland Yard.

All doubt is now removed regarding the identity of "Mr. John Robinson" and "Master John," who boarded the ship at Antwerp twelve days ago.

The very greatest precautions were taken to prevent Crippen from using his revolver either upon himself or the officers, and after the arrest was made the fugitive was not only closely watched by the four Canadian police, who accompanied the inspector, but they were reinforced by three of the Montrose's men appointed by Capt. Kendall.

Mr. Dew had communicated by wireless telegraphy to Capt. Kendall as he was coming up the river, requesting him to make certain arrangements, and these were carried out in every particular, so that the inspector's duties were given every chance of successful accomplishment.

The newspaper correspondents kept out of sight according to their agreement, which I previously cabled you, and there was nothing in the fact of the tug Eureka proceeding from the shore to the vessel to excite alarm in the fugitive, whose nervousness became more and more intense as he neared the ship's first stopping place.

UNDER COVER OF HEAVY FOG.

To him it must have appeared as an ordinary event in the routine working of the ship. He had been informed in casual conversation by Captain Kendall that at Father Point the pilot for the up-river journey would board, and that Customs officials would also be taken on at this place.

There was a fog early this morning, which was fairly thick all the way from here to the Gulf. It got a little thinner towards seven o'clock, but was moderately heavy when the Montrose arrived.

This circumstance was of great assistance to the police officers, who had a difficult task to accomplish, and doubtless lent a sense of security to the fugitives themselves.

About eight o'clock the deep tones of a steamer's whistle as she hooted her way up the river through the fog were heard answering the fog-horn at Father Point.

Instantly there was immense excitement among the anxious crowd here, few of whom had had any sleep all night.

In a few minutes Inspector Dew, accompanied by Chief McCarthy, of the Canadian police, and his assistants, appeared, and with police and newspaper correspondents in a condition of tense suspense the tug started out shortly after eight to meet the long-awaited Montrose.

DISGUISED AS A PILOT.

The inspector was disguised as a pilot and his face made up with seams which made him look like a weather-beaten "salt," and so effectually changed his appearance that none of us would have known him had it not been that he was the odd man.

The Canadian police were supposed to be Customs officials, but, of course, were not disguised in any way.

As we made our way out through the fog bets were offered and accepted as to the probability of the fugitives being the persons wanted, and excitement ran high.

The actual pilot was quartered below with the correspondents, and on the deck of the Eureka were visible only "Pilot" Dew and the four "Customs officers," all of whom were muffled up on account of the fog.

We had to drop down the river a little to meet the Montrose, which had begun to slow up.

When we got near enough to distinguish through the fog figures on her deck we saw the man who afterwards proved to be Crippen pacing up and down on the side we were approaching.

Capt. Kendall afterwards said that he had been nervously walking the deck since early morning, and anxiously looking toward the shore, striving to pierce the mist, in evident distress and alarm.

The boat swung round and approached the vessel from the other side, and Crippen, who appeared anxious not to be seen, did not follow with the rest of the passengers to witness the "coming aboard" of the pilot, but remained almost a solitary figure on the other deck.

At this time Miss Le Neve was in the cabin, which she had not left the whole morning.

"YOU ARE HAWLEY CRIPPEN."

It was close on to nine o'clock when Mr. Dew and his associates climbed up the ladders hung over the side for them.

The Inspector, accompanied by Chief McCarthy and his men, walked to the other side of the deck, where Crippen was, and as he turned the corner of the deck-house Mr. Dew encountered Crippen face to face.

"I want to see you for a moment, Crippen," calmly said Inspector Dew.

Though the man must have been taken frightfully aback, he showed no agitation whatever, and walked without making any protest to Captain Kendall's cabin. When they arrived there the Inspector said, "Mr. McCarthy, this is your man."

Chief McCarthy then said to him, "You are Hawley Crippen, and I have a warrant for your arrest on the charge of murdering and mutilating your wife."

Crippen, who was immediately seized by the Canadian officers, was on the verge of collapse.

Le Neve's arrest immediately followed.

[A Reuter cable says, "When Crippen saw the party come aboard he exclaimed, 'Isn't this unusual?' The surgeon who was walking on the deck with him did not reply. Mr. Dew walked past Crippen, and then, having made sure of his man, said, 'Crippen, I want you!' Crippen made no resistance, and was at once taken below and locked in a cabin with the Inspector."]

While this dramatic event was taking place on board the ship the rest of us clambered up the ladders to the deck, and awaited the advent of the inspector from the saloon.

The instant the arrest was made and the handcuffs slipped on Crippen the inspector had a wireless message flashed ashore.

It was a notification to Scotland Yard that he had succeeded in his mission, and arrested the man who was wanted for the crime since July 13.

This message was picked up by the Father Point station and hurried on its way to London by cable.

Meanwhile the Montrose kept under easy steam in order to hold her position against the tide, but made no move towards resuming her voyage.

Fifty correspondents are clamouring to use the wireless installation on the Montrose for the forwarding of messages to their respective papers, and I am allowed to send only this brief account at present.

This also will go by Father Point.

MISS LE NEVE'S TERRIBLE DISTRESS.

After the arrest had taken place in the captain's cabin Crippen was taken under charge of the police to his own cabin.

Here Le Neve sat, a pathetic figure, garbed in her boy's dress, waiting, fearing what might come, but not knowing what to expect.

The instant Inspector Dew entered the cabin with Crippen in custody of the Canadian officers, with handcuffs on his wrists, the girl started up in alarm, and looking with searching gaze at the inspector, she penetrated his disguise like a flash, and screamed, "That is Inspector Dew! Oh, what does he want?"

She sat quietly sobbing to herself for a few minutes, and then fainted.

Beyond declaring her innocence, she said nothing.

CRIPPEN EXPRESSES RELIEF.

Later both prisoners were closeted with Inspector Dew and Mr. McCarthy while the steamer got under way and proceeded towards Quebec.

We remained off Father Point not more than half-an-hour, and we are all now going on to Quebec in the ship to witness the final scenes of the two prisoners being charged before a magistrate in that city.

Chief McCarthy has just told me that Crippen said to him directly after his arrest, "I feel relieved. The strain of the past fortnight has weighed heavily upon me."

It is believed that Crippen has made some sort of confession, or at least an acknowledgment of the crime, without giving any details, but Inspector Dew, interviewed, said that he was not yet prepared to make any statement.

Illustration on the cover of a supplement to *Le Petit Journal* (Paris), 14 August 1910.

ARRESTATION DU DOCTEUR CRIPPEN ET MISS LE NEVE SUR LE PONT DU "MONTROSE"

Chief Inspector Dew

Poor Crippen was still in ignorance of the fate so close at hand. My pilot's uniform was proving an effective disguise. He had not yet recognized me.

"Good morning, Dr. Crippen," I said. The little man gave a start of surprise, and a puzzled look came into his eyes as they scanned me. For a second longer doubt and uncertainty were registered on his face. Then a sudden twitching of his Adam's apple told me that recognition had come to him.

Even though I believed him to be a murderer, and a brutal murderer at that, it was impossible at that moment not to feel for him a pang of pity. He had been caught on the threshold of freedom. Only twelve hours more and he would have been safely at Quebec.

"Good morning, Mr. Dew," Crippen replied, and his voice was as calm and quiet as it had been on the occasion of our first meeting at Albion House.

"You will be arrested for the murder and mutilation of your wife, Cora Crippen, in London, on or about February 1st last," I told him.

To this he made no reply, and offered no resistance as he was handcuffed and taken as unobtrusively as possible to a vacant cabin. An officer from Quebec (Inspector Dennis) was placed in charge and the door was locked.

Now for Miss Le Neve. Inspector McCarthy and I proceeded at once to the cabin she and Crippen had occupied. I knocked at the door and then walked in. Miss Le Neve was standing just inside, probably awaiting Crippen's return from his morning walk.

As I entered she looked up.

"I am Chief-Inspector Dew," I said formally.

There was no need for the introduction. It was clear from the frightened look in her eyes that she had already recognized me.

With a shriek she collapsed and would have fallen to the floor had I not caught and supported her.

I sent at once for the stewardess, a big pleasant woman, and with her assistance the unhappy girl was soon restored to consciousness.

Miss Le Neve as I had expected, was dressed as a boy in a neat dark-brown suit, and she looked the part reasonably well.

This was soon changed. I got the stewardess to lend her some female clothing, and stood outside the door while she changed into a woman again.

The clothes were not a good fit, but Miss Le Neve was very grateful. She had become tired of masquerading as a boy.

I told Miss Le Neve she would be arrested on a charge of murder, and cautioned her: "You are not obliged to say anything, but what you do say will be taken down in writing and used either for or against you."

To this she made no reply.

I then went back to Crippen, and read to him the warrant, and cautioned him in the same way. He also made no reply.

Next Inspector McCarthy and I carefully searched Crippen.

Pinned on his under-vest we found several articles of jewellery. These included a rising sun brooch, four rings, and a paste butterfly brooch....

He was then taken to another cabin, and on the way said: "I am not sorry; the anxiety has been too much." I then read the warrant in detail to him, but he made no reply. Inspector McCarthy then put the handcuffs on him.

Shortly afterwards Crippen said, "How is Miss Le Neve?" I said, "Agitated, but I am doing all I can for her." He said, "It is only fair to say that she knows nothing about it; I never told her anything."

Whatever may be said and thought about Crippen, one can only admire his attitude towards the girl who had shared his great adventure.

The reason for the manacling was that a calling-card and a piece of a similar card had been found in one of Crippen's pockets.

The card was printed:

> E. Robinson & Co.,
> Detroit, Mich.
> Presented by Mr. John Robinson

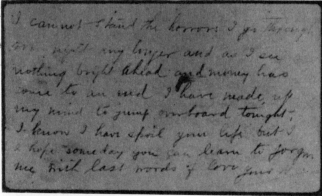

On the back of the card, Crippen had written in pencil:

I cannot stand the horrors I go through every night any longer and as I see nothing bright ahead and money has come to an end I have made up my mind to jump over-board tonight. I know I have spoilt your life but I I *(sic)* hope someday you can learn to forgive me. With last words of love. Your H.

On the back of the piece of card, he had written:
Shall we wait until tonight about 10 or 11 o'clock. If not what time?

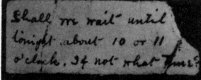

The *Daily Mail* of 3 August quotes the much-publicized solicitor Mr Arthur Newton as saying:

"I was on the eve of starting a short holiday when an old business friend of Dr. Crippen came to my office yesterday and asked me if I would undertake his defence, promising to do all he could to supply the necessary expenses for him".

Subsequently, it is revealed that 'the business friend in question was that prince of quacks Eddie Marr, alias 'Professor' Keith-Harvey, alias 'Professor' Elmer Shirley, alias W.S. Hamilton, obesity specialist. It is doubtful, however, whether Marr came to Newton's office in Great Marlborough Street, whose fittings were in green leather, and whose cigar cabinets were stocked with the choicest Havanas. More likely the solicitor sought out Marr in a shake-down operation designed to persuade Crippen's shady friend to cough up money for the latter's defence. The upshot was that Marr agreed to advance £100, and on the strength of this Newton sent the following cablegram to Crippen, then under arrest and held in a Quebec prison: "Your friends desire me to defend you and will pay all necessary expenses. Will undertake your defence, but you must promise to keep absolute silence and answer no questions and do not resist extradition. Reply confirming. Arthur Newton." Crippen, unaware of all of the backstage manœuvres, was only too eager to avail himself of Newton's services, and cabled accordingly, agreeing to all the latter's stipulations.

After being represented for a short time by a different solicitor, Ethel Le Neve also put herself in the hands of Arthur Newton.

FRIDAY, AUGUST 5, 1910.

WAS MRS. CRIPPEN POISONED?

MYSTERIOUS PURCHASE OF SUBTLE DRUG BEFORE THE TRAGEDY.

SENSATIONAL DISCOVERY.

PROF. PEPPER AND SCOTLAND YARD INVESTIGATING.

A sensational discovery of the purchase of deadly poison some time before the tragic death of Mrs. Crippen was reported to us late last night.

The police are investigating the purchase and the identity of the purchaser.

Meanwhile Crippen, acting presumably on the advice of his counsel, has become more taciturn.

He is regarded with evident aversion by his fellow prisoners, and takes his exercise when the yard is deserted.

He makes every effort to avoid the observation of the public, who can overlook the prison.

Miss Le Neve is in a much better physical condition.

The belief in her innocence grows.

We learn that the authorities are investigating an important piece of information which reached them a few days ago, and which may throw light upon Mrs. Crippen's death.

It has been discovered that a person made a purchase of poison on January 19 at the pharmacy of Messrs. Lewis and Burrows, 108, New Oxford-street.

The poison was hyoscin, a particularly subtle drug.

Five grains were bought. Half a grain is a fatal dose.

There is a suspicion as to who the purchaser was, and it is thought that if the police can confirm this belief it will go far to justify the theory that has been advanced as to how Mrs. Crippen came by her death.

A representative of "The Daily Chronicle" learned that the discovery was made by one of the staff employed by Messrs. Lewis and Burrows.

He at once communicated with Mr. W. E. Trick, J.P., who is chairman of the company, and that gentleman, realising the importance of the matter, decided to communicate with the police.

Before doing so he called the other members of the board of directors together, and informed them of the entry in the poison book, and the supposed identity of the purchaser.

It happened that one of the directors was acquainted with Professor Pepper, who is engaged upon analysis and investigation of the remains found in the house at Hilldrop-crescent. He therefore wrote that gentleman, giving him the particulars of the discovery.

Scotland Yard was also acquainted with the facts, and Superintendent Froest immediately entered into communication with Mr. Trick, with whom he had a prolonged interview.

There the matter rests for the present, but the investigation of Professor Pepper will now be to some extent based upon known data as to a possible poison.

Hyoscin is technically described as an alkaloid prepared from hyoscyamin by treating it with baryta water. Its hydrobromate is used as a sedative in mania and other forms of cerebral excitement.

The medicinal dose is from one hundredth to one two-hundredth part of a grain. So large a portion as half a grain would be most likely to prove fatal.

It closely resembles atropine (belladonna) in its action, but is more powerful.

It has a depressing effect generally acting on the central nervous system and paralyses certain glands of the heart.

MR. DEW LEAVES QUEBEC

Case Complete So Far as He is Concerned.

[Special Service Telegram.]

QUEBEC, Aug. 4.

Inspector Dew took breakfast early this morning and subsequently disappeared. Certain members of the provincial police expressed the opinion that the detective sought seclusion in order to avoid the annoyance of being obliged to deny the frequent but mostly quite erroneous statements attributed to him.

It was reported yesterday that Inspector Dew would go to Niagara Falls to-day, and this was taken to indicate that the case was completed so far as evidence from the prisoners themselves was concerned.

Mr. Dew's police associates point out that the English officer has practically nothing to do now but to wait until the process of the law should permit him to take the prisoners back to London.

Dr. Crippen is much changed in appearance since his arrival. The four days' growth of his beard has not improved his looks, and he is not allowed to shave.

Mr. Morin, governor of the prison, said that the precautions taken against the possibility of the suicide of Dr. Crippen were so strict that he was not even trusted in the hands of the prison barber.

The rumoured statements of Dr. Crippen in connection with the crime have sent correspondents scurrying from one provincial officer to another, and, although nothing in confirmation has been learned, it is variously reported that Dr. Crippen admitted having had a scuffle with his wife, after which she was seized with a fatal illness. He is also said to have explained that the death was accidental. To all such stories the police reply that so far as they know neither Dr. Crippen nor Miss Le Neve has made any statement regarding the crime.

Inspector Dew has not visited Crippen since yesterday morning, when he took the prisoner a fresh outfit from the scanty supply which the latter brought with him to Canada. To-day Crippen appeared in the prison corridor for the daily exercise dressed in these garments.

GOING BACK EARLY.

Governor Morin says that the authorities expect to get the pair off their hands by August 18 or August 19.

The time set by law for their detention on Canadian soil will expire at midnight of the 15th, and the first British steamer from here after that date sails on August 18. But there is a faster boat on the following day. The deportation may be postponed till the latter date.

Mr. Morin thought that the prisoners would not reappear before the Court, as the law governing their cases works automatically in the absence of any attempt to resist extradition.—Reuter.

MONTREAL, Aug. 4.

Advices from Quebec state that Inspector Dew is en route for this city to consult with Captain Kendall of the Montrose, and that he is expected to return this afternoon, after obtaining a written statement from the captain.—Reuter.

EARLY RETURN OF PRISONERS EXPECTED.

Detective-sergeant Mitchell and Wardresses Stone and Foster, from Holloway, arrived at Liverpool yesterday afternoon, and embarked on the Lake Manitoba, which sailed for Canada at 4.30.

Special arrangements have been made aboard the Lake Manitoba for the comfort of the party. Once on board, they proceeded to the saloon for afternoon tea.

Mr. Mitchell, who was seen on the ship by one or two members of the Liverpool detective force, stated that he did not anticipate any trouble with Crippen, but that it was necessary to have two officers on such a long journey, so that the prisoner could be watched night and day. For the same reason, two wardresses were being sent out.

The papers which Detective Mitchell is taking out will take a few days to put through at Quebec, and he said that as the time of departure from Canada of Crippen and Le Neve would probably synchronise with the sailing of the Lake Manitoba, it was possible the prisoners would be brought back on that steamer.

The proceedings would be conducted, he stated, in accordance with the terms of the Fugitive Offenders Act.

AUG. 7, 1910.   LLOYD'S WEEKLY NEWS.

THE CRIPPEN CASE

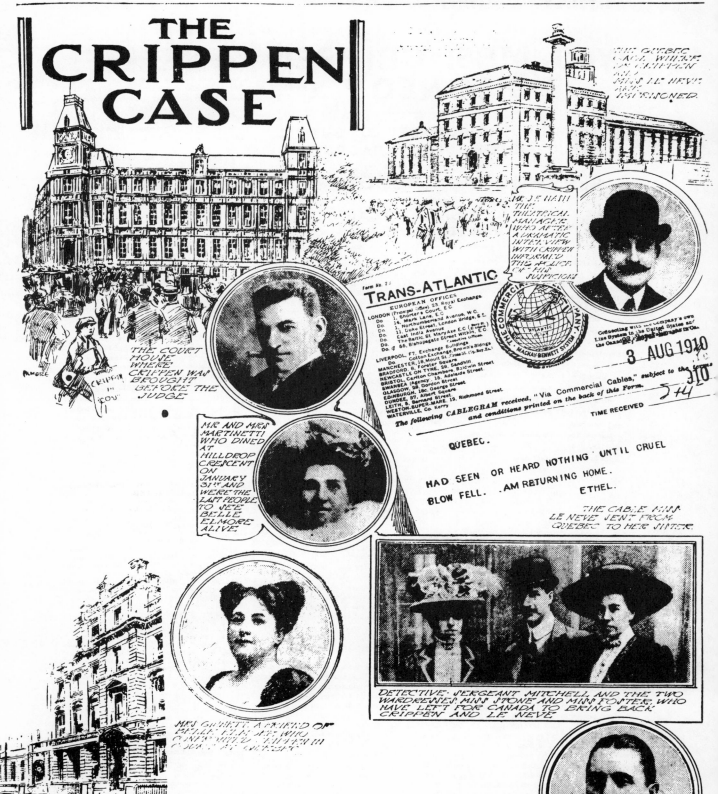

THE COURT HOUSE WHERE CRIPPEN WAS BROUGHT BEFORE THE JUDGE

MR AND MRS MARTINETTI WHO DINED AT HILLDROP CRESCENT ON JANUARY 31ST AND WERE THE LAST PEOPLE TO SEE BELLE ELMORE ALIVE

Trans-Atlantic

QUEBEC.

HAD SEEN OR HEARD NOTHING UNTIL CRUEL BLOW FELL. AM RETURNING HOME.   ETHEL.

THE CABLE MISS LE NEVE SENT FROM QUEBEC TO HER SISTER.

BOW STREET POLICE COURT WHERE THE CASE WILL FIRST BE HEARD IN LONDON

MRS GARRETT, A FRIEND OF BELLE ELMORE, WHO CONFRONTED CRIPPEN IN COURT AT QUEBEC

DETECTIVE-SERGEANT MITCHELL AND THE TWO WARDRESSES, MISS STONE AND MISS FOSTER, WHO HAVE LEFT FOR CANADA TO BRING BACK CRIPPEN AND LE NEVE

MR ARTHUR NEWTON, THE SOLICITOR WHO WILL DEFEND CRIPPEN

AUG. 7, 1910.   THE NEWS OF THE WORLD

CRIPPEN IN QUEBEC GAOL.

HIS INFATUATED SWEETHEART REFUSES TO MAKE A STATEMENT.

GRAPHIC STORIES OF FUGITIVES' LIVES ABOARD MONTROSE.

PRISONERS SEARCHED.

CANVAS HARNESS TO HIDE FEMALE FIGURE.

The prisoners having been secured, and the usual caution having been administered, the next thing was to search the prisoners. Crippen, of course, had no alternative but to submit. "I found," said Mr. Denis to a pressman, "no revolver and no knife—only £2, a small watch, and some trinkets. But"—and here Mr. Denis became very impressive—"he had a small phial filled with some sort of unknown liquid, and a folded paper containing a white, yellowish powder that looked very suspicious. I was glad that we had not wasted any time in putting the handcuffs on him." Inspector Dew, who was not satisfied with the results of the first examination, decided to make another search of Crippen. This time they went more carefully through his clothes, and were rewarded by finding that he had, with the aid of safety-pins, made a sort of belt of the lower part of his shirt. This was found to be a sort of treasure belt, containing three solitaire diamond rings, a large gold watch, a number of scarf pins, of no great value, and one ring set with four small diamonds and amethyst. The searching of the girl was a pitiful performance, but it had to be done. Miss Le Neve stood the ordeal well, but, as piece by piece they stripped her disguise from her, the tears came coursing down her cheeks every little while, and she wiped them away with her fingers. At times she held her head with her hand, a thumb and forefinger on each temple, as if her head were splitting. Her sole jewellery was a lady's solid gold watch and ring of little value. The money amounted to only £12, much of which was used later to purchase female clothing for her. She wore under her outer wearing apparel a sort of canvas harness, for the purpose of reducing her rounded form to the straight lines of a boy. To all questions put to her she merely replied "Yes" or "No," or remained silent. After it was all over, and Inspector Dew had advised her to

WEAR WOMAN'S CLOTHING

that would be provided her by one of the passengers she collapsed. At first she objected to doing so, but was at length prevailed upon to obey. The Montrose now got under weigh once more, and, with her passenger list reinforced by the police officials and the corps of pressmen from the Eureka, she weighed anchor and proceeded up the river to Quebec. As Crippen lay manacled in his bunk he complained of dulness, and asked to be allowed a book to read. It may have been some subtle humour that prompted the choice, but at any rate Crippen, the self-styled merchant and father, was presently engaged upon the "Letters of a Self-made Merchant to his Son." He lay huddled up in a corner on the couch, opposite the sleeping berths, with his handcuffed hands resting on his knees. When not reading he stared straight before him, with his prominent eyes starting, as it seemed, almost from his head. By and by the stare faded from his face, and he dropped asleep. Meanwhile, the doctor was in constant attention on Miss Le Neve, who remained trembling violently for hours. Later she became more composed, and tried, without much success, to read a magazine. There was something very pathetic about this, the end of her sorry masquerade, and the young girl in the borrowed dress of black and white check, and with shortened hair, was a sad enough figure. Her ill-fitting garments and tear-stained face added to the pathos of the fragile, lonely figure. Her hair was short cropped, unbrushed, and without a parting. As the vessel drew nearer to Quebec Inspector Dew entered her cabin, and was seen apparently pleading with her. The woman was sitting on a couch. It was after midnight. By her side sat Mr. Dew, talking very kindly yet firmly and persuasively. The woman sat with crossed legs, clasping her knee with her joined hands; hands that were very small, fragile, and feminine, not a bit like those of a boy of 18. Her head was turned upwards, and she stared hard at the ceiling as if torn by doubt, hesitation, and despair. A couple of hours later the vessel reached Quebec. Both she and Crippen looked exceedingly dejected when they were escorted off the boat. The girl had almost to be carried across the gangway. She wore a veil, mercifully lent her by a lady passenger to conceal her face from the scrutiny of bystanders. It was noticed that the only baggage the pair had with them was a hold-all, of the type known to Americans as a "grip," and a small handbag. The former bore a label with the address, "John Robinson, Detroit, Mich." Several cabs had been telegraphed for, and the prisoners, in separate conveyances, were driven off to the Parliament-buildings, to await the proceedings before the Quebec Court. In her desolate prison-chamber a further surprise and sorrow was awaiting the unfortunate girl. A cablegram for her had been received from her mother. It read:—

Darling Ethel,—With all the love you have for your husband, do not forget your father, mother, brothers, and sisters, and tell all you know to the authorities.

Miss Le Neve was so ysterical that the cable was not handed to her until some hours after her arrival, when she had regained some degree of composure. When she read her mother's message she again broke down. "Good God," she cried, "to think of the trouble I have given them. Oh! dear me, I wish I could die now and end it all. Later, in reply to a cable from her sister inviting her to explain everything and asserting belief in her innocence, Miss Le Neve cabled home:

I had seen or heard nothing until the cruel blow fell. Am returning home.—Ethel.

CRIPPEN IN GAOL.

PRISONER DUMB WITH DESPAIR AT HIS PLIGHT.

On board ship, after his arrest, Crippen was seen the picture of despair, his eyes fixed on vacancy, thinking, Heaven alone knows what bitter thoughts. A somewhat similar picture is presented of his life in his little cell in Quebec Prison. All he asks is something to read, and the prison authorities gratify him as well as they can. But the library is not a large one. Only two books were given him, one, "The Lives of the Saints," the other "The Annals of an Eventful Life." At his request these volumes were supplemented with a Bible. Crippen sleeps at night in a cell under constant observation, but it is small and not very comfortable, so he is allowed during the day to sit in the vestibule in charge of a warder. He still wears the shabby brown suit in which he landed from the Montrose. Mr. Morin, Governor of the gaol, told a pressman that Crippen sleeps fairly well, and that his appetite is good, but that he is taciturn, gloomy, and even morose, seldom speaking unless asked a question. It is said that his physical conformation lends support to the belief that he is a degenerate. On the day following his appearance before the magistrate Inspector Dew visited Crippen in his cell, and had a long conversation with him. There was no one else present, and after the interview Mr. Dew refused to give any information on the subject. Crippen was later permitted to receive the first message addressed to him from outside since his arrest. It was an invitation to make a public statement, and his reply was simply "No." The accused man will not be allowed to exercise in the hospital garden. He will be allowed to walk in the courtyard, which is surrounded by a very high wall. Wrapped up as he is in anxiety as to his fate, Crippen is not without curiosity as to what the world is saying of him. To one of the warders of the gaol, who personally look after him, he said, "What do people think of me?" but the warder did not enlighten him. About Miss Le Neve Crippen shows no curiosity.

BELLE ELMORE (MRS CORA CRIPPEN) IN A FAVORITE POSE

THE HOUSE WHERE MISS LE NEVE WAS BORN

INSPECTOR DEW

CHORUS OF THE SONG WHICH SO AMUSED CRIPPEN

MR. DAVE O'TOOLE ORIGINAL SINGER OF THE SONG, A CARICATURE AT THE VAUDEVILLE CLUB

THE "BOY" WHO USED SAFETY PINS AS BRACES.

It was the girl who betrayed Crippen. This is what the captain's most interesting story comes to. There was no disguising her figure, her manners, her voice, her general bearing. She was a girl all the time despite the boy's jacket and trousers. Not only the captain but some of the passengers out of the twenty-two in the first cabin, including four ladies, had their doubts about the alleged boy, and it is even probable that a few of the 214 steerage passengers were equally uncertain. "He did not look like a girl. He did not talk, eat, drink, walk, run, or play like a boy," the passengers said, "and on windy days, when the back of his sack coat was blown about and disarranged, one could see that his trousers were not suspended by braces, but by safety-pins." He had a little mincing gait, which easily awakened suspicions, he was too broad around the bust and too broad about the hips, too feminine in the arms and legs to be a boy. He had little mannerisms when with Crippen which were very womanly. Captain Kendall is a smart, handsome young officer, of 35, typically British in appearance, with light, curly hair, a fresh, weather-tanned face, keen grey-blue eyes, a light athletic frame, more suggestive of the soldier than the mariner, and clear-cut features. "When did you first suspect something strange about the couple?" a "Daily Telegraph" representative asked him. "Almost from the start," he said. "When we got to sea I did not at first notice the man so much as his companion. I thought 'Master Robinson' surely was a girl, and I said so. No, I didn't at once come to the conclusion that we had found the couple wanted, and when I was practically convinced in my own mind I still sought further proof. Fortunately, we had the description circulated by the London newspapers. The skipper, of course, also had pictures of Crippen and Miss Le Neve as they were generally known, the man wearing a moustache. He chalked out the moustache and the spectacles in the picture, for

CRIPPEN WORE NO SPECTACLES

aboard. The result was a likeness of "Mr. Robinson." "Here is something else I did," said the skipper, as he took from his desk a square of white cardboard, with a round hole cut in the centre and fitted it over a newspaper cut of Miss Le Neve. Thus super-imposed, it covered the girl's picture hat and dress, leaving only the face showing. "I did this and compared the pictured face with that of the passenger Crippen said was his son. The resemblance was striking. From close observation, by means of my cabin-window, which commands a fine view of the promenade deck, I gradually became convinced that my suspicions were correct. I carefully laid plans for getting bit by bit all the evidence possible for their identification. After allowing for the alterations which anybody desirous of disguising oneself could easily adopt, I found that the descriptions printed tallied almost exactly, all excepting on one point. Scotland Yard said that Miss Le Neve was 5ft. 5in. in height, but the 'Robinson' boy was shorter by an inch. I talked the matter over with our chief engineer, Mr. Viner, and we both concluded that the police had got a wrong idea of the woman's height because they had not allowed for a woman's high heels and topknot on her head. Put Miss Le Neve into a man's shoes, cut her hair as short as she wears it to-day, and the difference of one inch disappears. For a time I was puzzled how to learn whether Crippen really had false teeth. My plan was to encourage the man's confidence, to answer his questions about the ship and matters at sea, and to try to make him quite at home. I think I succeeded. We both got quite at home very shortly" —and the captain smiled sardonically. Crippen was invited to the captain's cabin, and all the old chestnuts Capt. Kendall had ever heard were raked out for his benefit. "You see," continued the captain, "I wanted the man to

LAUGH RIGHT OUT AND SHOW HIS TEETH

and he did laugh several times quite heartily, and then I knew indeed that the teeth were false.

CRIPPEN IN THE CHORUS.

FUGITIVE ENJOYS SING-SONG WITH FELLOW PASSENGERS.

Though Crippen did not like Miss Le Neve to be embarrassed with the polite attentions of their fellow-travellers, he himself was cool enough to join to some extent in the ordinary recreations of life on a liner. Always fond of music, he sometimes attended the concerts held during the voyage, and once, at all events, joined with gusto in the chorus, and laughed heartily at a passenger's rendering of "We all walked into the shop" (published by Messrs. Francis, Day & Hunter). Here are a few of the verses which tickled the "doctor's" sense of humour :—

We passed a little laundry, where
    We got our washing done.
Said Brown, "There's plenty of girls in here
    "Come in, we'll have some fun."
            Chorus
    So we all walked into the shop
        To shelter from the rain,
    They wanted to iron my dimples out,
        So we all walked out again.

Inside a big confectioner's
    We saw a big display
Of pastry there, and a ticket said,
    "Our tarts are cheap to-day."
            Chorus
    So we all walked into the shop
        To shelter from the rain,
    We ordered some tarts with jam inside,
        Then we all walked out again.

We heard a fellow shouting, just
    Outside a penny show.
"Walk up! and visit the big fat girl
    Who came from Borneo."
            Chorus
    So we all walked into the shop
        To shelter from the rain,
    We gave her a penny, and pinched her arm,
        Then we all walked out again.

THE NEW YORK TIMES, SUNDAY, AUGUST 7. 1910.

A TRANSALANTIC CHASE WITHOUT THE WIRELESS OR CABLE.

THE spectacular transatlantic chase of Dr. Crippen, accused of the murder of his wife in London, made by Inspector Dew of Scotland Yard, which resulted in his capture on Sunday last—a chase of many days with the fugitive unknowing, the pursuer unrelentless, and the world looking on, recalls another very similar pursuit across the Atlantic's wide expanse made by Inspector Tanner of the same force in the early sixties, and his apprehension of Francis Müller, before landing in New York, who was suspected of having killed Thomas Briggs in a first-class compartment of a train on the North London Railway.

This crime startled two continents and held the people's interest at fever heat for many weeks, quite as the Crippen case has done both in this country and abroad. In the Müller case it was the nemesis of steam—its supremacy over the sail that was the murderer's undoing, while in the matter of Crippen wireless telegraphy acted as the goddess of vengeance, but the pursuit and capture in 1864—for that period—was just as exciting as the one that ended a week ago.

Late in the evening of July 9, 1884, a passenger entered one of the first-class compartments of a train pulling in at Hackney station, not far from London, but its condition caused him to make a quick retreat; for the interior showed plainly that a deadly struggle had taken place there and some sort of a crime had very evidently been committed. The place was literally besmeared with blood

It was only a few hours afterward, however, that the body of a man, terribly beaten and cut, and later identified as Thomas Briggs, 60 years old, chief clerk in the banking house of Roberts, Curtiss & Co. in Lombard Street, London, was found lying near the tracks of Wick station, not many miles away. He died in a few hours without giving a statement or description of the murderer.

For days the police were nonplused. To work on so slender a clue as a hat, that was found not to belong to Mr. Briggs, and to succeed in locating its owner in the hundreds of thousands of London's population, seemed almost an impossibility. But they kept at it just as they did in the Crippen case.

The first information that pointed directly to any one individual as a suspect was furnished by the little daughter of a cab driver who lived at Bow.

Behind him, in his room, the youngster found a small cardboard box, such as jewelers use, and upon showing it to her father he remembered reading that the name on the box—that of a jeweler named Death—it was, indeed, more than significant, as the box was the first real clue—was the tradesman who had received in exchange a chain identified as belonging to the murdered man. Subsequently Mr. Death identified a picture of Müller, which he had given to the cab driver's daughter, as the man who had exchanged the chain for another.

The cabman then recalled, too, that Müller had in his possession a fine gold watch, but was very reticent as to how he came to have it. Finally he ceased to wear it, and accounted for this by saying that it had been taken from him in a brawl, yet he refused to advertise for it or to even try to locate the parties whom he said he suspected of stealing it.

Then followed the argus-eyed efforts of the British police and Scotland Yard to locate the German, and by their persistence, even in the face of great difficulties, it was learned that a man answering his description had taken passage some days previous on a sailing vessel named the Victoria, bound for New York. Already he had many days' start, but it was figured that the passage of the sailing craft would occupy about nineteen days before it reached American waters, and there was just a chance of getting him before he landed in America.

The matter was placed in the hands of Inspector Tanner, who, after obtaining a warrant for Müller's arrest, sought for some means to beat the fugitive in his race across the Atlantic. There were no five-day steamers in those days.

The Government was appealed to, and Sir George Grey offered every facility, and with the result that within a few hours after it was known that Müller had probably sailed, Inspector Tanner, Sergt. Clarke, Mr. Death, and the cabman were on an Admiralty steamer hot on the trail of the alleged murderer, who, they had every reason to believe, was on the Victoria bound for New York, :

It was figured that the Admiralty steamer would arrive in New York some few days before the Victoria—as a matter of fact, the steamer did cast anchor on Aug. 5, but at that time there had as yet been no word as to the whereabouts of the sailing ship. Upon arrival, Inspector Tanner communicated with the British Consul and Chief Kennedy of the New York Police Department and steps were taken at once to insure prompt notice of the arrival of the Victoria ,

For this purpose the Sandy Hook Telegraph Company was instructed to immediately forward any information of the incoming vessel to Police Headquarters and to the Quarantine Station, where Inspector Tanner and his party were waiting. The Secretary of the pilot officers also communicated with the various pilots telling them to keep a sharp lookout for the Victoria and a reward of $25 was offered to the first pilot who boarded that vessel

A few days passed and the Victoria entered the lower bay. The picture is much the same as the arrival of Crippen at Father Point.

After boarding the sailing vessel and their mission made known Capt. Champion, as a ruse, ordered all the passengers forward on deck for examination by the health officer. Inspector Tanner was the health officer in this case. Müller was among them, and was quickly recognized by Mr. Death and the cabman. He was seized immediately.

"What is it?" he cried, and when told he was wanted for the murder of Thomas Briggs, turned ghastly pale.

"I did not do it," he shouted. "I can prove that I was not there at all!"

The murderer was turned over to the United States authorities, extradition arranged for, and Inspector Tanner and his prisoner left for home on the Etna, the officer with probably the same amount of satisfaction as that with which Inspector Dew returns with Crippen and his girl companion. The party reached London Sept. 17. Müller was very quiet during the trip—said little or nothing other than to protest his innocence.

It took but a few days to convict Müller, who still persisted that he was not guilty, and he was sentenced to death on Oct. 31. During the trial he conducted himself with considerable dignity. The proof against him was wholly circumstantial, and the result of this was that in Germany the feeling against the British Government ran high, for Müller's fellow-countrymen believed him innocent, and his simplicity, apparent gentleness, and the truthfulness of his statements of innocence appealed to many even in London. When a verdict was found against him and sentence passed he arose and quietly said:

"I am at all events satisfied with the sentence which you have passed. I know very well it is that which the law of this country prescribes. What I have to say is that I have not been convicted on a true statement of facts, but on a false statement."

After this many more people were inclined to think him guiltless. The time came for his execution. The date was Nov. 1, 1864,

The condemned, marvelously calm, walked briskly to the scaffold, and as he sat on a stool awaiting the adjustment of the rope that was to swing him into eternity he repeated in German the words the minister uttered, "Christ, the saint of God, have mercy upon me."

Dr. Cappell, the attending physician, said to him: "In a few minutes, Müller, you will stand before God. I ask you again, and for the last time, are you innocent or guilty?"

"I am innocent," Müller replied.

Then Dr. Cappell repeated it after him in the form of a question—"You are innocent?" and to which he responded, "God Almighty knows what I have done."

"Does God know that you have done this particular deed?" queried the physician. And then, after weeks of endeavor to have him make a confession to a crime which the authorities were morally certain he committed, Müller came out with the truth and said: "Ich habe es gethan," meaning "I have done it."

The physician and minister muttered "Thank God!" and the execution proceeded, the trap was sprung quickly, and Müller paid the penalty of his crime the details of which, the reason for it, and all that will never be known.

Franz Muller

This picture, or one like it, seems to have inspired the following oddly-shaped verse:

Miss Le Neve, old Dew is waiting on the wall for you at Liverpool,
And he says he saw you sitting on the knee of Doctor Crippen,
Dressed in boy's clothes, on the Montrose, Miss Le Neve.

Comments from the actor-manager Seymour Hicks (husband of Ellaline Terris – whose father, the matinee-idol William Terris, was murdered outside the 'royal' rear-entrance of the Adelphi Theatre, London, where he was starring, in December 1897):

'I knew Crippen personally but not well. On the first occasion that I met him I spent half an hour in his company at the Vaudeville Club . . . . I am bound to say that I never hope to have the privilege of drinking with a milder-looking or more gentle little murderer. Crippen was short, slightly built, of pale complexion and was possessed of fair hair, a quantity of which had played truant. The most noticeable thing about him was his eyes. They bulged considerably and appeared to be closely related to some kind of ophthalmic goitre. Added to this, as they were weak and watery he was obliged to wear spectacles with lenses of more than ordinary thickness, which so magnified his pupils that in looking at him I was by no means sure I was not talking to a bream or mullet or some other open-eyed and equally intelligent deep-sea fish. He spoke with a slight American accent. I fancy I should have forgotten him altogether had it not been that on this particular afternoon he presented the acquaintance who had introduced us with one of Munyon's Remedies, assuring him that it would instantly relieve the acute toothache from which he was suffering. This kindly action on the "Doctor's" part enabled my friend to recall him to my mind when he said to me, some two years afterwards, "Would you believe it, they've arrested Crippen for murdering his wife. You remember him, the little patent-medicine fellow I introduced you to who gave me a cure for toothache." This fact earmarked the occasion, and it is not unnatural that it flashed across my mind that he had evidently prescribed something entirely different for the peroxide beauty who, in addition to giving him her hand, had probably given him the devil of a time after the marriage ceremony . . . . He numbered among his friends many music-hall artists, and it was Marie Lloyd, that Queen of music-hall comediennes, who nicknamed him "the half-crown king". It appears he was always short of this particular coin of the realm and made a habit of borrowing it whenever possible. His usual procedure was to invite a friend to have a drink with him and then, finding to his dismay that he had come out without any money, say, "I'm so sorry. Would you mind lending me half-a-crown?" Not only did two-and-sixpence enable thirst to be quenched but the change found a home in the "Doctor's" pocket.'

LLOYD'S WEEKLY NEWS

SPECIAL SUNDAY EDITION.   CIRCULATION OVER 1,350,000.

No. 3,536. REGISTERED AT THE G.P.O. AS A NEWSPAPER.   LONDON : SUNDAY. AUG. 28, 1910. Entered as Second-Class Matter at the New York, N.Y., Post Office, 1903.   ONE PENNY.

CRIPPEN AND MISS LE NEVE ARRIVE IN LONDON.

CROWDS HOOT THE HEAVILY-MUFFLED PRISONERS AS THEY DRIVE FROM EUSTON TO BOW-STREET POLICE STATION.

DRAMATIC ATTACK ON THE DOCTOR.

MYSTERIOUS YOUNG MAN RUSHES AT HIM WITH A STICK, AND IS HUSTLED AWAY BY POLICE.

"Dr." Crippen and Miss Le Neve returned to England yesterday, landing at Liverpool from the White Star liner Megantic early in the afternoon, and travelling to London by the boat train.

The arrival at Euston was marked by a public demonstration, crowds booing them as they were hustled into taxi-cabs and hurried to Bow-street.

They will be formally charged at Bow-street Police Court early to-morrow morning, having reached London too late last evening for the purpose.

A dramatic scene marked the landing at Liverpool, a young man rushing forward to attack Crippen. A scrimmage took place, in which the police indiscriminately hustled the public away from the prisoners.

The prisoners are spending the week-end in the cells at Bow-street, to await their appearance before the magistrate to-morrow morning.

STARTLING INCIDENT.

[From Our Special Correspondent.]

LIVERPOOL, Saturday.

With one intensely dramatic episode, lasting but half-a-dozen seconds, "Dr." Crippen and Miss Le Neve this afternoon landed in England again, to answer charges in relation to the death of Belle Elmore, the music hall artist, whose mutilated remains were found in the house until recently occupied by her husband.

Detective-Inspector Dew, of Scotland Yard, with his colleague, Sergeant Mitchell, were on the White Star liner Megantic, and were joined at the mouth of the Mersey early in the forenoon by Chief-Detective-Inspector Duckworth, of the Liverpool force, who went out in a tug with instructions to place his services at the disposal of his London colleagues.

Exactly as the gun-fire from the fort announced the hour of one, the white deck and railings and khaki-coloured funnel of the steamer came into sight opposite New Brighton, and five minutes later she was swinging round in the tow of a powerful tender, preparatory to coming alongside.

At ten minutes past two the last of the 160 first and second-class passengers had boarded the boat train in Riverside Station, and everything was ready for a start. Up to that moment no one could ascertain where the Crippen party were, or what were the plans for conveying the two prisoners to London.

The disembarkation of the Canadian troops who travelled by the boat and of the ordinary passengers had been made by the forward gangway from the second promenade deck, but I had earlier noticed another very insignificant and unobtrusive gangway pushed out, linking one of the steel doors in the vessel's side at the very stern of the ship with the landing stage, and when everyone else was comfortably seated in their carriage on the London train Inspector Dew and his colleague, with their prisoners following behind, walked rapidly across the gangway and landing stage and dashed for the door of the Custom House shed, which was hastily opened.

INSPECTOR DEW'S MISTAKE.

So far everything had gone smoothly, and, with the exception of the soldiers and police, not a dozen people noticed the little party. But Inspector Dew had made one mistake. He had muffled Crippen's head and face and drawn his hat low over his eyes, and thereby labelled him as plainly as if he had been ticketed.

With dramatic suddenness, and with set teeth, a tall young fellow dashed at Crippen with uplifted cane, and in a second there was a knot of fighting uniform and plain clothes officers and civilians. The officers spared no one. They just threw themselves upon the rushing crowd of people, battling almost savagely, and driving them back towards the water and along the landing stage.

It was an intensely dramatic exhibition on the part of the man—who declares that he had no direct personal interest in the parties—of uncontrolled and passionate hatred. No one else joined in it, and but for hoarse shouts of "Get back there. Away you go out of it," by the police, the silence was almost oppressive.

Crippen's face was scarcely visible, but a glimpse of his eyes in the fraction of a second revealed a terror-stricken gaze. His eyes seemed to stand out with fear.

Inspector Dew half led, half pushed him through the door of the shed, which was shut in the face of all who tried to follow

except one or two of us, who were so mixed up with officers and prisoners as to be swept in with them.

Inside the shed no time was wasted. The party passed at once across the shed, and through a door opening on to Prince's Parade, which was kept free of people by two lines of police. Walking hurriedly, and with an anxious glance by Crippen to right and left, the party crossed the Parade, passed through another door on to Riverside Station platform, and entered their compartments.

From that moment no one except holders of special permits or steamer tickets for London were allowed upon the platform, and by 2.20 p.m. the train was on the move en route for Willesden and London.

As the train moved away the blinds were drawn at the windows, and uniformed men, who had taken up a position near the door, moved off, thankful that their task was accomplished.

Miss Le Neve, who had almost hidden her features in a blue veiling that was almost black in its density, appeared to bear the ordeal of the hurried departure and attack better than her companions. She sank into her seat obviously ill and worn by the prolonged strain.

On the voyage, as I learned later, she had stood her trouble well and bravely, accepting anything that was done for her comfort with grateful thanks, and giving no trouble.

So the long chase and return journey has closed, and amidst the strains of a military band playing welcoming tunes in honour of the Canadian troops, Crippen has gone back to London to defend himself against the most serious charge known to law.

The whole story of his home-coming would be amusing if it were not so tragic. On Friday night nothing was known here for certain, except the fact that Inspector Dew and his party were on board the Megantic, and that the ship would arrive about noon. Whether the party would land in Liverpool or drop off by tug elsewhere was not known even to the Liverpool police.

During the night, however, a strong breeze from the north-north-west sprang up, and by eight o'clock this morning the rough condition of the water at the mouth of the river and in the estuary made it almost certain that it would be impossible for a woman to be safely taken off before reaching the landing-stage.

In spite of this some of the watchers went out on tugs to meet the vessel, fearing lest some way might be found of depriving them of the sight they desired more than most things. But had we known, there was no need for any such measures. Inspector Dew had decided to adopt the simplest and most obvious course. When the vessel came near enough to be searched with glasses he could be seen on deck, in company with Chief Detective-Inspector Duckworth standing fully in view. From the steamer end of the gangway he watched the Canadian troops and passengers leave. Then he disappeared, as we knew later, for the purpose of moving his party aft for the carrying out of his plan. The after-gangway was not used except by a very few officials of the White Star Line having business on board. One or two of us made an attempt to follow, but the gangway was lifted a couple of feet at the landing stage end.

LINES OF TROOPS.

In the meantime, under pretence of making room for the troops, the people were pushed back behind a line of police standing almost shoulder to shoulder. Then the Canadian troops were lined up two deep in front of the police, and finally the moveable hydraulic gangway was brought forward somewhat, so as to further obscure the view. General Bethune, who was in charge of the military reception, was right away near the bows of the ship, talking with Sir Henry Pallatt, and public, pressmen, and photographers were also at the end. Suddenly forms appeared at the dark opening in the ship's side, the gangway fell again with a thud, and Mr. Dew, with his prisoners and colleagues, passed out into daylight.

It was cleverly done, and Mr. Dew will, on the whole, deserve congratulation. Had the troops not impeded his passage for a single second, he would have passed into the shed practically unobserved. As it was, the soldiers had to break line to let him pass, and some of them got jostled in the scrimmage.

Passengers who made the journey on the Megantic tell me that they saw practically nothing at all of either prisoner. " Now and again, but always at night," said one, " I saw one or both of them on the boat deck, but it was always too dark to distinguish their faces. It appeared to me that the prisoners were never allowed to get near each other while exercising, and I don't think they ever had a chance to speak to each other. Once one of the officers met Miss Le Neve and the wardress in the gangway, and, mistaking the two ladies for friends in the half light addressed a bantering remark to them as to 'notorious' fellow-passengers. The one whom he afterwards knew to be Miss Le Neve turned sharply away and ' glared at him as if she would destroy him with a glance.' "

The Press Association states that Crippen was seasick during the gale which the vessel experienced on Thursday, and he is not in very good health. Miss Le Neve, however, is in good spirits, and was laughing heartily previous to the disembarkation.

ARRIVAL IN LONDON.

Crowds Hoot the Prisoners as They are Swiftly Driven to Bow Street.

Thousands of spectators loudly hooted " Dr." Crippen and Miss Le Neve when they drove out from Euston Station last evening on their way from Liverpool to Bow-street. There was no attempt on the part of the crowd to discriminate between the two prisoners. The scene was pathetic in the extreme, and while some of the onlookers were extremely outspoken in their condemnations, others were obviously touched by the pitiful appearance of the two figures in the sensational drama.

When the train that conveyed them from Liverpool steamed into No 1 platform of the London and North-Western terminus, only a few privileged persons were within the barriers that had been erected by the station officials and the police. Beyond that enclosure, on every platform and at every position that could command a view, thousands of people were gathered in expectation of some sensational occurrence. They 'must have been grievously disappointed. They saw only two drooping, pathetic figures, a man and a woman, who were hustled out of the train, hurried across the platform, and bundled into the waiting taxicabs in which the party, prisoners and custodians, were driven off at top speed to Bow-street Police Station.

" Dr." Crippen wore a long grey coat that reached down almost to his heels, and this, with a large soft felt hat, marked him out from the smartly dressed police-officers who had him in charge.

" What a tiny little man he is," remarked several of the spectators, contrasting the shrinking figure of "Dr." Crippen with the stalwart detective officers who surrounded him. Crippen did indeed look tragically pitiful to those who got a glimpse of him in his rush across the platform to the waiting taxicabs. His clothes seemed too large for him, and he made himself look smaller than he is by bending his head almost on to his breast.

Miss Le Neve was an even more pathetic

H. H. CRIPPEN

figure. She wore a long dark cloak, and was heavily veiled, and, like her companion, she seemed to feel her position keenly.

In their hurried rush across the platform, they both kept their heads bowed, as if anxious not to meet the gaze of the officials on the platform and the public beyond the barriers. Crippen especially seemed nervous, and when he found himself on the station platform, he seemed positively to shrink from the men who were gathered round about him, charged with his safe delivery into the hands of the law.

When he heard the angry shouts of the crowd, he cast a quick, furtive glance on one side, and, if anything, quickened his pace across the platform.

Miss Le Neve, closely veiled, showed greater courage, and marched erect from the train to the cab. The first outburst of indignation from the crowd seemed to take her aback, but her ordeal did not last more than a few seconds.

The train which conveyed them from Liverpool reached Euston at eleven minutes before seven, or about nineteen minutes behind scheduled time. Long before that, every approach to Euston Station was lined with spectators anxious to catch a glimpse of the prisoners, women being in the majority.

BITTER RECEPTION.

The railway officials had cleared No. 1 platform fully an hour before the time when the train was due. A strong barrier was erected opposite a spot which had been marked out as the position where the compartment in which Crippen, Miss Le Neve and their custodians travelled would draw up. A second barrier had been erected further on, and between these two and at the precise spot marked by the officials, the carriage duly pulled up.

A special police force, about 100 in number, had been drawn up beyond the barriers, and no member of the public was admitted, so that, until they reached the outer gates of the station, it was a painfully silent reception that awaited the "Doctor" and his companion. Not a word was spoken by those immediately concerned, but beyond the barriers and on the other platforms there were the waiting thousands, who began their hostile demonstration. Groans and hooting broke the silence, and it was obvious that the man and the woman were taken aback by the outburst. They shrank closer to their custodians, and it was painfully evident that they could not get too speedily away from the station.

The police managed the arrival at Euston and the removal to Bow-street with remarkable cleverness. Anticipating an immense crowd at the station, they made their arrangements accordingly, and the two prisoners were got away from the station with as much alacrity and as little opportunity for a display of feeling as was possible.

In the train the blinds of the carriages had been drawn, so that the identity of the occupants in the saloon immediately behind the engine could not be guessed. The same precaution was taken when Crippen and Miss Le Neve were bundled into the taxi-cabs. In the first cab was Inspector Dew, Detective-Sergeant Stephens, and Crippen. Miss Le Neve travelled in the second, with Sergeant Crutchett and two prison warders. In the third there were Inspector Kane and Sergeant Cornish.

Leaving by a side gateway, the three vehicles turned into Seymour-street, to the intense disgust of a long line of spectators, who had assembled in Drummond-street. Passing down Seymour-street, the cabs crossed the Euston-road, where there was a great gathering of people.

MISS LE NEVE IN TEARS.

Passionate Interview with Her Sister Last Night at Bow Street.

By special permission of the police authorities, Mrs. Brock was allowed the privilege of an interview with her sister, Miss Le Neve, almost immediately after her arrival at Bow-street.

The interview which took place in the police-station, lasted only a very few minutes. No mention whatever was made of the tragic circumstances which had brought Miss Le Neve a prisoner, nor of the voyage from Quebec.

Seen at her home by a representative of " Lloyd's News," Mrs. Brock said :
" I saw her in a special cell in the presence of a policeman and a wardress.

" We were both too full of emotion for words. She came to my arms and lay there for a minute or two while we kissed each other. I need hardly say how glad I was to see her, even under these circumstances.

" Ethel looked pale and white. Her cheeks had sunken since I saw her last in July. Traces of the worry and strain she had undergone were evident on her face. When she spoke first her lips quivered slightly, but she bore up well. Indeed, considering the circumstances, she was wonderfully bright, though there was deep sadness apparent in her manner and her voice. I was afraid at one moment that she would break down, but the pleasure of seeing me evidently kept her up.

" I had her god-daughter—my little girl—in my arms, and Ethel was overjoyed to see the child, for whom she has a great affection.

' She took the child in her arms, and kissed it passionately.

" She asked after her brother-in-law, and sent her love to him and to her nephew, whose photograph I showed her."

COMMITTAL PROCEEDINGS AT THE BOW STREET MAGISTRATES' COURT, 6 SEPTEMBER 1910

A MORNING LEADER ARTIST'S SKETCHES IN COURT . . . . .

MR TRAVERS HUMPHREYS OPENS THE CASE FOR THE PROSECUTION

MR ERNEST HEWART PAWNBROKER'S ASSISTANT

MRS MARTINETTI FRIEND OF MRS CRIPPEN

DR CRIPPEN

MISS LE NEVE

MISS MAY - SECRETARY

DR HERBERT BURROUGHS FRIEND OF THE CRIPPENS

THE ACCUSED IN THE DOCK

BOW ST 6 SEP -10

DR. WILLCOX

DR MARSHALL WHO WAS SHOWN THE REMAINS

PROFESSOR PEPPER GIVES HIS EVIDENCE FOR THE CROWN

SIR W·S·GILBERT — A SPECTATOR, FROM THE BENCH.

HAROLD KIRKBY CHEMISTS' ASSISTANT

BOW STREET MAGISTRATES' COURT

Most of the witnesses portrayed by the *Morning Leader* artist have been referred to in earlier reports. Among those who have not been mentioned or who have been mentioned only in passing, EDGAR BRETT, assistant manager of the Charing Cross Bank, Bedford Street, Strand, gave details of the Crippens' joint current and deposit accounts; MARION CURNOW, manageress of Munyon's Remedies, Albion House, Oxford Street, since 1 February 1910 – when Crippen's connection with the firm ceased – stated that at the beginning of March 1910 Crippen gave her two envelopes to keep in the office safe, and subsequently told her, 'If anything happens to me, please give what you have there to Miss Le Neve' (when the envelopes were opened by the police, one was found to contain bank deposit notes and insurance receipts, and the other a brooch and a woman's watch), and that on 9 July she cashed a cheque for £37 for Crippen, having noted that it bore the signatures of himself and his wife, and having looked at his pass-book, which showed a balance of £37 and a few shillings; ERNEST HEWART, an assistant at Attenboroughs, pawnbrokers, 142 Oxford Street –

where, on 2 February 1910, Crippen pawned a marquise diamond ring and a pair of diamond earrings for £80, and a week later pawned a diamond brooch and six diamond rings for £115; HAROLD KIRBY (not Kirkby), an assistant at Lewis & Burrows, chemists, 108 New Oxford Street, gave evidence of the sale of a narcotic poison to Crippen on 19 January 1910, and 'proved' the entry in the poisons register – '*Name of purchaser*, Munyons, per H.H. Crippen. *Address of purchaser*, 57-61 Albion House. *Name and quantity of poison sold*, five grains of hyoscin hydrobromide. *Purpose for which it is required*, homœpathic preparation. *Signature of purchaser*, H.H. Crippen'; GILBERT RYLANCE stated, inter alia: 'I carry on business as a surgeon-dentist under my own name at Albion House. I met Dr. Crippen for the first time about the middle of 1907. In 1908 I started the business of The Yale Tooth Specialists at Albion House, and Dr. Crippen became my partner. About March of this year I entered into a fresh agreement with him. Dr. Crippen agreed to put £200 into the business, and I was to put in my experience, knowledge, and skill. We were each to have half profits. I remember seeing Mrs Crippen about 26 January of this year. I heard from Dr. Crippen about 1 or 2 February that she had left. This letter, which is written on my own headed paper, is dated 9 July 1910:

'Dear Mr Rylance, – I now find that in order to escape trouble I shall be obliged to absent myself for a time. I believe with the business as it is now going you will run on all right so far as money matters go. Plucknett's last account you will find in my desk. As to rent, you have only to send Goddard & Smith £10. 12s. 6d., as I have already paid them £30 off £40. 12s. 6d. (this is in advance up to Sept. 25). If you want to give notice you should give six months' notice in my name on September 25, 1910. Long knows pretty much all the business, and can take over the book-keeping. There will be several paid bills to enter on my file in my desk, the key to which you will find in the upper drawer of the little cabinet in Coulthard's office. I shall write you later on more fully. With kind wishes for your success. Yours sincerely,

H.H. Crippen.

'Mrs Crippen's death was announced as having taken place on 23 March – two days before Good Friday – and about a fortnight or so later he told me that he had married Miss Le Neve.'

The parts played in the investigation by DR. AUGUSTUS PEPPER, consulting surgeon at St. Mary's Hospital, and DR. WILLIAM WILLCOX, senior scientific analyst to the Home Office, are explained by L.A. Parry, MD, BS, FRCS:

The organs found in the cellar (the heart, the lungs, the windpipe, the gullet, the liver, the kidneys, the spleen, the stomach, the pancreas, and the intestines) were all typically human. It was not possible, on

MRS HARRISON IDENTIFIES CERTAIN GARMENTS

CHIEF INSPECTOR DEW PRODUCES AN ERMINE CAPE

MR EDGAR BRETT OF THE CHARING CROSS BANK

MISS CURNOW

"A MORNING LEADER" ARTIST'S SKETCHES IN COURT

AMONG THE SPECTATORS

MRS JACKSON. MISS LE NEVE LANDLADY

MR LONG WHO SAID HE PURCHASED A BOY'S SUIT

MR NEWTON ASKS BAIL FOR MISS LE NEVE

MR GILBERT RYLANCE, DENTIST

anatomical grounds, to determine the sex of the victim. The only parts which could definitely settle that, the organs of generation, were completely missing. But buried with the remains were some Hinde's curlers with hair in them belonging to a woman, and some woman's vest and combinations, which were evidence that the remains were almost certainly those of a female.

Whose were the remains? Perhaps the most important discussion arose in connexion with a piece of flesh and skin with a mark on it. The police, after consultation with eminent medico-legal experts, said that it came from the lower part of the abdomen and that the mark was the scar of an operation. If this were correct, it went far to prove that the remains were those of Belle Elmore,

for it was demonstrated by Mrs. Martinetti, an old and intimate friend of Mrs. Crippen, that in 1909, when she was staying at her bungalow on the river, she saw, whilst Belle Elmore was undressing, a mark on the lower part of her stomach. It was right in the middle and seemed to be the mark of an old cut. It was darker than the rest of the stomach and was about six inches long. She only saw it once. She had made some remarks to her about it. The defence would urge that the so-called scar was not a scar at all but a mark made by the folding of the skin.

Dr. Pepper gave a report to the police on his findings. He was quite definite on the matter. He recognized from anatomical data that the piece of skin submitted to him was from the lower part of the abdominal wall. He spent several hours in examining the mark on it and came to the positive conclusion that it was a scar. It was just in the position that the scar of an operation for the removal of the female internal organs of generation would occupy, and those organs were completely absent in the remains. Although he had not the slightest doubt from his naked-eye examination that the mark was a scar, he spent some time and considerable care in making sections and examining them under the microscope. The fact that the remains had been in the ground some time did not, in his opinion, materially accentuate the difficulty of making certain that he was dealing with a scar. Part of the mark was without question of a different nature and was due to pressure and folding of the skin. The fact that in a perfect scar there could be no hair follicles or sebaceous glands, and yet that there were in the sections of this scar both of these, simply meant that the scar was not quite perfect, a tiny piece of skin had got included in it. This was by no means an unusual event. The scar was not quite perfect. It was nearly an inch wide at the bottom and tapered off to about a quarter of an inch at the top. This was quite a usual thing to happen in a scar, especially in this position. He was unable to find any definite stitch-marks, but this, too, was not unusual when a scar had stretched and spread out to the width of this one. The navel was often removed in an operation and its presence or absence was not of any importance. Another reason which made him so sure that the piece

of flesh was from the lower part of the abdomen, was that there was a line of hair which he believed was pubic.

Dr. Bernard Spilsbury also made an examination and report for the police. On several occasions he saw the piece of skin and flesh with the mark on it and he also was decided in his view that it came from the lower part of the abdomen. The row of short dark hairs, which he regarded as pubic hairs, confirmed his conclusion. He made a careful examination of a section of the skin where the mark was. This was undoubtedly scar tissue. There were no glands in it, but in a section of the other part of the skin where there was a mark which he regarded as due to folding there were glands. If a few glands were found in a scar this would be accounted for by the imbedding of a tiny piece of skin.

DR. THOMAS MARSHALL, police surgeon for the Kentish Town district, confirmed the opinion of the other two doctors. He regarded the piece of skin as from the lower abdominal wall, and as being marked by a scar. The three experts were in complete agreement that the flesh examined was from the abdomen and that it was scarred. This proof that there was a scar on the body in the position where Belle Elmore had a scar, together with the circumstantial evidence afforded by the various articles found buried with the remains, was practically conclusive in identifying them as those of Cora Crippen.

Dr. Pepper examined the portion of a woman's combinations found with the remains. It was found to be of cotton. This was the kind of garment worn by Mrs.

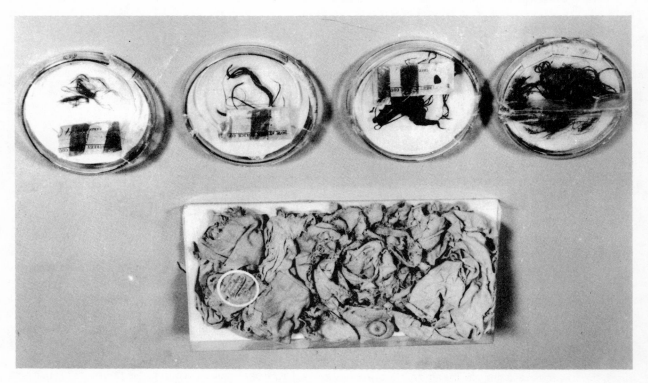

Police specimens showing the remains of a pyjama jacket bearing (encircled) the Jones Brothers label. The hanks of hair include one (second from left) still in a Hinde's curler.

Crippen. His examination of the part of a pyjama jacket, found buried in the cellar with the parts of the body, showed that there was a collar with a label on it, "Shirtmakers, Jones Brothers (Holloway) Limited, Holloway, N.", and on referring to the collars of the jackets of the two suits of pyjamas found by Inspector Dew at Crippen's house, he found that the labels were the same. The buttons on the two sets of garments, those found in the house at Hilldrop Crescent, and those buried in the cellar, were of the same make. The hair in the Hinde's curlers was from two to three inches long, was dark brown in colour, shading off to light brown, and had been dyed. It was that of a woman.

The buyer at Jones Brothers was able to recognize the piece of pyjama found in the cellar as bought from his firm, which had not become a limited company till 1906. The proof that the pyjama coat was sold in 1908 at the very earliest disposed of the contention that the remains found in the cellar had been placed there many years before Crippen had entered on his tenancy, which was in the year 1905. It was also a strong presumptive point in favour of the remains being those of Crippen's wife. This was considerably strengthened by the testimony of MRS. ADELINE HARRISON, an old friend of Belle Elmore of more than twelve years' duration, who was able to state, in connexion with the articles found buried with the remains, that she knew that the hair of the deceased was dark brown when she first became acquainted with her. Afterwards she bleached her hair so that it altered in colour. The hair found in the Hinde's curlers was similar to that of Mrs. Crippen as she had seen it early in the morning, before it was curled. She also recognized an undervest which was found among the remains as exactly like the undervests worn by Mrs. Crippen.

The time at which any remains have been buried is very difficult to arrive at, the stage of decomposition depending on many accessory circumstances, such as the nature of the soil, the dampness or dryness of it, and so on. In this case, all the experts were able to say was that the time they had been in the ground was from four to eight months, and as Crippen had been the tenant of the house for over four years, the possibility that the remains had been interred in the cellar before the commencement of his tenancy, was disposed of.

The next step in the investigation was to determine in what manner death had been brought about. A very careful examination of the remains, which it must be remembered included most of the vital internal organs, but not any of the organs of generation, and not the head or limbs, showed that they were quite normal, and not in any way diseased. There was nothing in this examination which revealed any natural cause for the death. There was no evidence of violence, no cut, stab, or gunshot wound, or any other injury. But it must be recalled that as the head and limbs were missing, the absence of evidence of injury was no proof that Belle Elmore had not died a violent death. However, acting on the assumption that there had not been any wound

or similar cause to account for death, the experts naturally proceeded to search in the remains for the only other likely cause, namely poison. The means employed were long, difficult, and complicated, and it is not necessary to enter into them in minute detail, but a brief account of the processes adopted will be instructive and useful.

On 23 July, Dr. Willcox commenced to examine some of the viscera for poison. He received from the coroner's office five jars. In the first there was a small part of the liver and one kidney; in the second, a pair of combinations; in the third, hair in a hair-curler, a handkerchief, and undervest, and some hair in a piece of paper; in the fourth, a piece of pyjama jacket; and in the fifth, two other pieces of a pyjama jacket, one piece having a button on it, and the other having a neck-piece on it with a tab. This array of articles shows the thoroughness with which the police had collected anything which might help them to determine the cause of death, and also definitely determine the exact nature of the portions of clothing found. In addition to the jars already detailed, later the following were sent to Dr. Willcox: one containing a part of the liver and some intestine, and another a hair-curler with hair in it. He first of all searched for the mineral and inorganic poisons. Dr. Willcox found traces of arsenic in the liver and intestines, but this was of no importance, it was in very small amount and was accounted for by the disinfectants which had been employed by the police to lessen the odour of the decomposing remains. He then looked for the common alkaloids (the essential principles of the organic poisons). The more usual, such as morphine, strychnine, and cocaine, were first searched for. In the remains under examination none were found. Then the more unusual bodies were looked for and there was found an alkaloid which dilated the pupil when put into the eye of a cat. There are two varieties of pupil-dilating alkaloids, the most usual, the vegetable, and the rare, the animal. Dr. Willcox used a test called Vitali's test, which by a colour reaction showed him he had found a vegetable alkaloid. There are three vegetable pupil-dilating alkaloids (excluding cocaine, which he had proved by other tests was not present), and therefore he had now arrived at the fact that he was dealing either with atropin, hyoscyamin, or hyoscin. Further tests showed him that he had found hyoscin. In the whole of the organs which he analysed there were two-fifths of a grain, which would mean more than half a grain in the whole body. The effects of hyoscin are as follows: First there is a little delirium and excitement, the mouth and throat become dry and then quickly the patient becomes drowsy and unconscious and completely paralysed, death resulting in a few hours. The patient does not recover consciousness.

Dr. Willcox mentioned the fact that the animal pupil-dilating alkaloids were produced in the process of putrefaction of dead animal matter. He applied the test of Vitali. This test when used with a vegetable alkaloid turns it purple violet, gradually fading away to brown, but it has not this colour reaction with an animal alkaloid. This is characteristic of all three vegetable pupil-dilating alkaloids, and therefore, does not settle which of them it is. Further tests are necessary for the determination of this point. They were carried out by Dr. Willcox.

Dr. Arthur Pearson Luff, honorary scientific adviser to the Home Office, confirmed the opinion and findings of Dr. Willcox.

This was the first case in which murder by poisoning with hyoscin had ever been charged. Hyoscin is one of the two alkaloids found in henbane leaves, the other being hyoscyamin. The former is salt and bitter in taste; this is easily disguised by tea, coffee, beer, stout, or spirits. When used in medicine, which is quite rarely, it is generally given by injection under the skin, in doses of $\frac{1}{100}-\frac{1}{200}$ grain. It is employed in a limited number of cases of nervous diseases such as mania, delirium, meningitis, and delirium tremens, sometimes for insomnia, or as a sedative. As a rule a medical man would only use it extremely rarely. In homœpathic practice it is not used at all. It will be remembered that Crippen had been connected with Munyon's, which dealt in such remedies. He attempted to explain his purchase of a large quantity of this drug by saying that he wanted it for use in his business.

The police-court proceedings went on sporadically until 21 September, when the magistrate ordered that the prisoners be tried separately, Crippen for murder, Ethel Le Neve as accessory after the fact.

The separateness of the trials would be increased by the fact that Crippen insisted to his legal advisers that Ethel should not be called as a witness on his behalf.

Drawing of the henbane plant, from which the poisonous alkaloid hyoscin is extracted.

The last of Dr. Willcox's fifteen pages of notes.

Hyoscine Hydrobromide (or the salt of Hyoscine) is a very powerful Narcotic poison and in large doses ($\frac{1}{2}$ grain or upwards) it will produce at first some delirium and stupor with dryness of the throat and paralysis of the pupils. Very soon complete unconsciousness and coma with paralysis will follow and in a few hours death will result.

The relatively large amounts of the poison found in the stomach and intestine shows that it was taken by mouth. The amount present in the liver and kidney shows that the deceased probably lived some little time – an hour or more – before death occurred.

Sept 2/10   W.H. Willcox, MD

CORONER'S ORDER FOR BURIAL.

(To be issued only upon an inquest being held.)

I, the undersigned, Coroner for the _County_ of _London_ Do hereby authorise the Burial of the Body of _Cora Crippen alias Belle Elmore_ late of _39 Hilltop Crescent Islington_

aged about _____ which has been viewed by the Inquest Jury.

Witness my hand this _26th_ day of _September_ 19_10_

Walter Schröder Coroner.

SEE NOTICE ON OTHER SIDE.

Trial of
Hawley Harvey Crippen

THE CRIPPEN CASE.

4,000 APPLICATIONS FOR TICKETS FOR TO-DAY'S TRIAL.

Over four thousand applications have been received for admission to the Crippen trial, which begins at the Old Bailey to-day, but only 700 tickets have been issued, and most of these are for the use of those having business in court. The tickets for the public are half-day ones. The trial is expected to last four days, and eight series of seventy half-day tickets have been issued.

A large crowd is expected to gather in the vicinity of the court in the hope of seeing the arrival of Crippen and the various notable people engaged in the trial, but it is probable that the City Police will clear the adjacent thoroughfares.

Crippen will be put on trial at 10.30 this morning. As already announced, the prisoners will be tried separately, Crippen being charged with murder and Miss Le Neve only with being an accessory after the fact. Should Crippen be acquitted, Miss Le Neve will automatically be acquitted also.

The jury will, of course, be kept locked up until their verdict is given, the Sheriffs providing accommodation for them at an hotel.

CENTRAL CRIMINAL COURT,
OLD BAILEY, LONDON,

TUESDAY, 18th OCTOBER, 1910.

Judge—

THE RIGHT HON. LORD ALVERSTONE, Lord Chief Justice of England.

Counsel for the Crown—

Mr. R. D. MUIR,
Mr. TRAVERS HUMPHREYS, and
Mr. INGLEBY ODDIE.

(Instructed by the Director of Public Prosecutions.)

Counsel for the Prisoner—

Mr. TOBIN, K.C.,
Mr. HUNTLY JENKINS, and
Mr. ROOME.

(Instructed by Messrs. Arthur Newton & Co.)

THE DAILY GRAPHIC, WEDNESDAY, OCTOBER 19, 1910.

PUBLIC INTEREST IN THE TRIAL OF "DR." CRIPPEN.

THE GREAT CROWD GATHERED OUTSIDE THE CENTRAL CRIMINAL COURT, WHERE THE PROCEEDINGS OPENED YESTERDAY.   INSET: MR. R. D. MUIR, WHO OPENED THE CASE FOR THE PROSECUTION. ("Daily Graphic" photograph.)   (See page 7.)

THE CRIPPEN TRIAL IN PICTURES.

(1) Dr. Crippen (marked with a x) arriving at the Old Bailey. (2, 3, 4, and 5) Drs. Marshall, Spilsbury, Pepper and Willcox, the medical experts for the prosecution. (6) The jury on their way to court (inset, the juror who fainted during the trial). (7) Mr. Bruce Miller, an actor friend of Mrs. Crippen. (8) Mrs. Martinetti. (9) Inspector Dew.

SIR RICHARD MUIR'S NOTES FOR THE PROSECUTION

These notes were described by another lawyer, Mr Louis Blom-Cooper, as 'a model of how any counsel might provide himself with the signposts for conducting a case'.

I am reproducing here Muir's own version of the case against Crippen as he prepared it in readiness for the prosecution. It is, I think, the first time that such a document has been published in its entirety :

HAWLEY HARVEY CRIPPEN,
M.D. HOSPITAL COLLEGE,
CLEVELAND, U.S.A.
48 years of age.

Agent and Manager for
Munyon's Remedies, Albion House
Advertising Business
Tooth
Eye
Ear remedies.

Cora Crippen
" Belle Elmore "

1900	Music Hall Singer
1906	of Brooklyn, U.S.A.
3 Sep. 1873.	About 37 years of age
1892/3.	Marries Crippen as his second wife.

Comfortably off,
lived at 39 Hilldrop Crescent,
£50 p.a.

21 Sep. 1905.

Well furnished
Latterly kept no servant.

Life together.

On affectionate terms
Kind & attentive husband.

Contrast Crippen's statement
" Ungovernable temper "
" Often threatened to leave me "
" Not co-habited since 1906 "
Boasted of attentions from other men
e.g. Bruce Miller.

In Fact Crippen carrying on
an intrigue with his typist
Ethel Le Neve for 3 years.
She had been typist to Crippen
for 8 years.

Money.

Crippen says he provided all
the money for the
home.

If so
For four years he had been
supporting a wife for whom
he had no affection.

A lady with expensive
tastes in furs, jewellery
& clothes.

While for three of those
years his affections were
fixed upon another woman,
with whom he " frequently
stayed at Hotels " but " was
never away from home at
night."

The wife during this time was
threatening to leave him
saying she was fond of another man
receiving love letters from another man
seeming to think Crippen not good
enough for her
saying she had a man to go to and
would end it all.
Not easy to tolerate by a husband if
such a state of things really existed.

FINANCIAL POSITION
31 Jan. 1910.

15 March, 1906.	Between them had put by £600
24 March, 1909.	on deposit at Charing Cross Bank.
Nov. 1909.	Crippen ceased to draw £3 weekly Became sole agent but it did not pay.
15 Dec. 1909.	Notice to withdraw deposits by (Cora Crippen) Belle Elmore on Dec. 15, 1910.
31 Jan. 1910.	Connection with Munyon's ceased.
31 Jan. 1910.	Crippen had other businesses but doubtful if any of them a source of income then.

Certain that current account with
Charing Cross Bank then overdrawn
£2. 7. 8.

Clearly pressed for money.

MOTIVE.

Belle Elmore
stood between him
and the closer relations he
wished to establish with Ethel
Le Neve

Belle Elmore's
money (and other
property convertible into money)
would enable him to keep Ethel
Le Neve.

31 Jan. 1910.
Invitation
Twice repeated to Mr. and
Mrs. Martinetti to dinner.

4 and 6 p.m.	
8 p.m.	Dinner party.
1 Feb. 1.30 a.m.	

The Martinettis witnesses to
the affectionate terms on
which husband and wife
then were.

1 Feb. 1910.

noon.   Crippen called and inquired
for Paul.
How is Belle ?
A. " All right."
If Crippen saw her that
day no one else
did.
Cora Crippen
never seen again.

DISAPPEARANCE OF CORA CRIPPEN.

Heaps of friends
England and America
Some relations there.

37 years of age
> Best of Health and spirits
> Bright, vivacious,
> Fond of life
>> dress
>>> jewellery.
> A good correspondent
Never heard of again.

Passed out of the world which
> knew her
> as completely as if she
> were dead.

Left behind her
> everything she would
> have left behind her
if she had died on that
day :
> Money
>> Jewels
>>> Furs
>>>> Clothes
>>>>> Home
>>>>>> Husband.

Would she return ?

Never to Return.

Crippen's certainty.

He very early made up his mind that
it was certain she would not return.

He immediately appropriated her
property :

2 Feb.   Pawned
> Pair of earrings &
> Marquise Ring for £80.

9 Feb.   Pawned
> Diamond Brooch and
> 6 diamond rings for £115.

20 Feb.   Gave to Le Neve
> Brooch " Sunrise "
> Fox Furs.

12 March.   Took Le Neve to live in the house
> 39 Hilldrop Crescent.
The house which had been Belle
> Elmore's home.
But he did not tell Cora Crippen's
> friends
>> They had parted for ever
>> She would never return.

He started a campaign of lies
> to account for her disappearance.

The Music Hall Ladies' Guild.
> Hon. Treasurer
> Cheque Book—Deposit Pass Book
> Meetings Wednesday.

If missing inquiries

Anticipated by Crippen

1 or 2 Feb.   Letter to Guild (cheque and deposit books enclosed)
Letter to Miss May, the Secretary.
> " Illness of a near relative
> calls me to America at
> a few hours notice.
> Cannot spare a moment to
> call upon you before I go."

Those lies told—at her request
> To cover up the scandal
> the best way he could with
> their mutual friends and Guild.

The man who
> went to Ball where mutual
> friends and Guild were.
With his typist
> wearing his wife's jewels.
Took the typist to live with
> him at his wife's home.
Seen about with her
> dressed in wife's furs.

To account for her
> not coming back.

Invented letters from relatives in
> California saying Belle was
> ill.

A letter from Belle saying not to
> worry as she was not so bad.

20 March.   A cable—dangerously ill with
double pleuro-pneumonia.

23 March.   If anything happens to Belle would go
to France for a week.
> (in fact going to Dieppe for Easter
> with Le Neve).

24 March.   Telegram from Victoria Station
" Belle died yesterday at 6 o'clock."

25 March.   Good Friday.
Death advertisement in " Era "
" to prevent people asking a lot of questions."

Easter.   Visit to Dieppe with Le Neve.

March 23—in California, U.S.A.
Miss Belle Elmore
(Mrs. Crippen)

INQUIRIES BY FRIENDS.

Mrs. Martinetti & Mrs. Smythson
> asked a lot of questions
> & extracted some answers.
She died at Los Angeles, Cal.
Her relations with her
His son saw her die
> Son's address given.
Wreath useless because to be
> Cremated.
> Ashes to be brought over
can have ceremony here.

18 May.   He had the Ashes at home.

Wanted to know the name of
the boat she sailed in to
America.

Must have been obvious to
Crippen that his statements
were being doubted.

Mr. Nash called on Crippen
Nash had been to America
had tried to find Belle Elmore
or get news of her and
had failed.

30 June.   Nash went to Scotland Yard
and saw Chief Inspector Dew.

INQUIRIES BY POLICE.

Dew made inquiries and then
8 July.   called at 39 Hilldrop Crescent.
10 a.m.   Found Le Neve there
> went with her to Crippen's
> business address.

Albion House

Dew said Mrs. Crippen's friends were not satisfied as to the stories Crippen had told about his wife's death.
Dew had himself made exhaustive inquiries and he also was not satisfied.

Did Crippen desire to offer any
    explanation.
Crippen must have seen it was useless to
    persist in the story he had told up to
    then, which had been inquired into and
so he said :
" I suppose I had better tell the truth.
    It is untrue what I have told them about
    her death. So far as I know she is still
    alive."

He then made a statement which was written down and signed.
In it he accounts for his wife's disappearance in quite a new way.

1902. While Crippen had been away from
    her in America she had
    formed an attachment for a
    music-hall artist named
    Bruce Miller.

Since his return she gave way to ungovernable
    outbursts of temper in which
    she threatened to leave Crippen
    and join Bruce Miller

She said that when she left him
    she would go out of his life
    altogether and he would never
    hear from her again.

31 Jan.
1.30 a.m. Because he did not show Mr. Martinetti
    to the lavatory she, after the
    guests had gone, had one of those
    outbursts of temper.

She abused Crippen.
    She said that was the finish of it—
    She would leave him to-morrow and
    he would never hear from her
    again.
    He was to arrange to cover up the
    scandal with their mutual friends
    and the Guild the best way he could.

1 Feb.
5 or 6 p.m. Went to business
    Returned—found she had gone
    Sat down to think how to cover
    up her absence without any scandal
    So wrote to the Guild etc.
        but
    Realized this would not explain her
        non-return
        so
    Told people she was ill and
        afterwards that she was dead, and
    advertised her death in " Era "
    to prevent people asking a lot of
    questions.

    Why he told lies.
Those lies were told at her request
    " to cover up the scandal
    the best way he could
    with their mutual friends
    and the Guild."

    By the man
        Who went to the Ball of the Music
20 Feb.   Hall Benevolent Fund with his
        typist wearing his wife's brooch
        where mutual friends and members
        of the Guild were certain to be
        met.

12 March. Who took the typist to live with
        him in what had been his wife's
        home.
    Who had been seen about with his
18 May.   typist wearing his wife's furs.

What ever his reason for telling those lies
It was not to cover up scandal.

Crippen said his wife left jewellery
    behind and took the rest with
    her.
He had never pawned anything of hers.

Two reasons for her disappearance :
(1) Because he did not show Mr. Martinetti to the
                lavatory.

(2) To join Bruce Miller.
(1) Too trivial to require comment.
(2) Untrue in fact.

PREPARATIONS FOR FLIGHT.

Envelopes had been deposited with Curnow in safe.
8 July.   " Know nothing about things in safe.
4 p.m.   If anything happens to me—
        Give it to Le Neve."

9 July.   Crippen was early at office
        Sent Long to buy boy's clothes.

    Cashed a cheque for £37 through
        Miss Curnow.

11.30.   Le Neve seen at the office
1.   Crippen seen by Rylance and Long
    for last time.

4.15.   Posted letter to Long
    " Wind up my household affairs."

Also posted a letter to Rylance
    " To escape trouble I shall be obliged
    to absent myself for a time."
Hands over business to Rylance to continue or not as he pleases.

FLIGHT.

9 July.   Police circulated a description
        of Mrs. Crippen.

11 July.   They went to Albion House
        to Hilldrop Crescent
Crippen was gone
Le Neve was gone
Neither of them seen again by police
31 July.   until they were found on board a s.s.
    off Quebec.

Crippen disguised by the shaving
    of his moustache
    passing under a false name
    and
Le Neve with him on the s.s.
    disguised as a boy.

What had Crippen to fear
    if Cora Crippen was alive ?
What would he have done
    if he believed she was alive ?

He had nothing to fear but
    he fled
        he disguised himself
        he used a false name
He took Le Neve with him
    disguised as a boy
He said he would do all he could to get
    in touch with her.

He would have advertised for her
        but he left the advertisement
        which he had prepared
        behind him.
Did he believe she was alive.

From what had Crippen fled ?

11 July.   The police searched the house at
        39 Hilldrop Crescent.
        They found the advertisement which might
        have been Crippen's salvation
        if Cora Crippen was alive—
        derelict—in one of the rooms.

At Albion House
        a suit of Crippen's clothes and
        Le Neve's hat
        Signs of the flight but nothing
        to account for it
        until

13 July.   Human remains were found in the cellar
        of 39 Hilldrop Crescent.

A hole had been dug in that cellar:
        the human remains put into it
        and the brick floor relaid.

Whose remains were they ?

14 July.   They were examined in the cellar by Dr. Pepper
        and Dr. Marshall.
        They and some things found with them
        were removed to a mortuary.
        Since then they have been submitted
        to a critical examination.

They were
                headless
                        limbless
                                boneless
        and practically all indications
        of sex had been removed.
        There remained only
        some of the viscera and some
        pieces of flesh.
Sex.
(1) Could not be determined with certainty on
    anatomical grounds.
(2) Some Hinde's curlers with long human hair and
    some feminine undergarments indicated a woman

On the other hand there were parts of a man's
pyjama jacket and a large handkerchief which
was probably not a woman's.

Identity.
(1) The hair was brown and had been bleached.
    Belle Elmore's hair was brown and had been
    bleached.
    That was no doubt true of other women besides her.

(2) The undergarments were such as
    Belle Elmore
    and no doubt such as many
    other women wore.

(3) Flesh :
        A piece of the lower abdominal wall and
        bearings—an old scar was among the
        remains.
        Belle Elmore had had an
        abdominal operation
1892 or 1893.   which had left a scar.

(4) Stout :
        The remains were those of a
        rather stout person.
        Belle Elmore was rather stout.

(5) Age :
        The remains were those of an adult
        person of young or middle age.
        Bell Elmore was 37 about.

3 Sep. 1873.

(6) Time of burial :
        The remains had been buried from 8 to 4
        months giving a wide margin.
        Belle Elmore disappeared 1 Feb. and the
        remains were unearthed on 13 July
                                —5¼ months.

(7) Place of burial :
        Belle Elmore was last seen alive in
        that house

    Who put those remains into
                        the ground ?

Opportunity :
        Crippen since 21 Sep. 1905 was
        tenant and with Belle Elmore
        sole occupiers.

Mutilation :
(1) Done by person having
    some knowledge of and some
    dexterity in the anatomy of
    human beings or other animals.

    Crippen had a medical
    training
    Had practised in
    America
    Attended hospitals in
    England to see operations.

(2) Would require time and
    security from
    interruption.

    Crippen was alone in
    that house on and after
    the 1 Feb.

Carrying :
        To place such remains as
        those in the hole
        prepared for them
        would require something
        in which to carry them.
        A pyjama jacket would
        serve that purpose.

(3) Pieces of pyjama jacket were
    found with the remains. It was
    probably a whole jacket
    when put there.

There are grounds for saying that
that jacket was Crippen's.

The Grounds :
(1) On 14 July Chief Inspector Dew
    found in a box under a bed in
    39 Hilldrop Crescent 3 pairs of
    pyjama trousers and 2 pyjama
    jackets forming two suits and
    one odd pair of trousers.

    The jackets are marked on a label
        Jones Brothers {on the
        Holloway.   {neck part.

(2) The pieces of pyjama jacket found with
    the human remains correspond in material
    and pattern with the odd pair of
    trousers.

(3) One piece—the neck part—is marked
    on a label
            Jones Brothers
                    Holloway Road.
    identical.

(4) One piece with a button identical.

Arrest.

Chief Inspector Dew
          having received information
boarded the s.s. " Montrose " in the R. St.
Lawrence near Quebec and before she had
arrived there from Antwerp.
Crippen had shaved off his moustache.
He had assumed the name of John Robinson
          of Detroit, U.S.A.
In the same ship
      occupying the same cabin was
          Ethel Le Neve
      disguised as a boy—hair short
      wearing the brown suit bought
      by Long on 9 July by Crippen's orders.

Chief Inspector told Crippen he would be arrested
for the murder of his wife and cautioned.
Crippen said nothing in answer.
      Later he said :
          " I am not sorry ; the anxiety
          has been too much."

He was searched—two cards were found on him. One
intended apparently for Le Neve had written upon
it : " I cannot stand the horrors I go through
      every night any longer and as I see nothing
      bright ahead and money has come to an
      end I have made up my mind to jump over-
      board to-night.   I know I have spoilt your
      life but I hope some day you can learn to
      forgive me. With last word of love. Your H."

Chief Inspector McCarthy put handcuffs on Crippen.
Chief Inspector Dew said :
          " We must put these on
      because a card found on you
      you have written that you intend
      jumping overboard."

Crippen said :
          " I won't. I am more than satisfied
      because the anxiety has been too
      awful."

Crippen was searched and while
      that was being done by Dew
Crippen said :
      " How is Miss Le Neve ? "
Chief Inspector said :
      " Agitated but I am doing all
      I can for her."
Crippen said :
      " It's only fair to say that she
      knows nothing about it.   I
      never told her anything."

Sewn to undervest :
      4 rings.
      " Rising Sun " brooch.
      " Butterfly " brooch (paste).

Voyage to England.

20 Aug.   Sailed on s.s. " Megantic."

21 Aug.   Warrant read—Crippen said : " Right "

24 Aug.   Crippen said :
        " When you took me off the ship I
        did not see Miss Le Neve.
        I don't know how things will go ;
        they may go all right or they may
        go all wrong with me.

        I may never see her again and I want
        to ask if you will let me see
        her—but I won't speak to her.
        She has been my only comfort for
        the last three years."

He did see Le Neve in the train between Liverpool
          and London.

27 Aug.   Charged at Bow Street Police Station.
          Said nothing.

21 Sep.   Committed—" Not Guilty—no witness."
Opportunities to give explanation of his
          flight
    31 July. On arrest.
    21 Aug. Warrant read.
    27 Aug. Charged at Bow St. Police Station.
    21 Sept. On committal.

Summarized Facts.

Motive on 31 Jan.

Disappearance of Belle Elmore.

Crippen only person who professes
      to account for that disappearance.

His first account admittedly false.

His second account followed by immediate
          flight.

Human remains found in the
      house in which she was
      last seen alive.

Pyjama jacket missing from
      Crippen's pyjama
      suits.

Pieces of the missing jacket
      found with the human
      remains.

The remains mutilated by
      some one having the opportunity
      and the anatomical knowledge
      Crippen possessed.

Cause of Death.

Post Mortem :
      Revealed no cause of death.

The viscera were submitted to
      Dr. Willcox
      Senior scientific analyst to Home Office.

He examined them :
   (1) for Mineral and organic poisons and
      found arsenic and Cresol, carbolic and
      Sanitas fluid.

   (2) Made extracts for the purpose of
      detecting alkaloids.

   (3) Tested the extracts for alkaloids
        Stomach ⎫
        Intestine ⎬ Found Alkaloid
        Kidney ⎪
        Liver   ⎭

   (4) Tested for different kinds of Alkaloids
      Found one of the vegetable Mydriatic
      Alkaloid and it was either
Deadly Nightshade   (1) Atropine
                 (2) Hyoscyamine
Henbane   or
                 (3) Hyoscine

   (5) Tested to see which of those three it was
      Atropine   ⎫ are both
      Hyoscyamine ⎭ crystalline.
      Hyoscine does not crystallize but
          forms a gummy residue.
      Bromine test.
      Atropine   ⎫ under " Bromine Test "
      Hyoscyamine ⎭ give small brown
          crystals
          but
      Hyoscine gives small brown spheres.

The result of those tests was that Dr. Willcox found in the viscera a quantity of hyoscine sufficient to show him that in the whole body there must have more than half a grain of the drug " Hyoscine Hydrobromide " the form in which hyoscine is sold and used for medicinal purposes.

Hyoscine Hydrobromide
is a powerful
narcotic poison
not commonly prescribed,
used as a sedative
in cases of mania, delirium,
delirium tremens or meningitis,
occasionally also as a hypnotic
in small doses of insomnia.

$\frac{1}{100}$ to $\frac{5}{200}$ part of a grain is the official dose.

If a large dose were taken
very quickly
drowsiness and
complete unconsciousness
and paralysis would follow
and death within a few hours.
$\frac{1}{4}$ to $\frac{1}{2}$ a grain is a fatal dose.

Dr. Willcox
therefore found in this body
indications that more than a
fatal dose of this deadly poison
had in some way been taken.

Moreover.
He found that the distribution
of the poison indicated that
(1) it had been taken by the mouth.
(2) the person lived an hour or more.

He found nothing in the viscera to account
for death
except hyoscine
and in his opinion
the cause of death
was poisoning by hyoscine.

CAUSE OF DEATH.

Remains would not have been
buried where they were
unless death caused by
unlawful criminal means.

Remains would not have been mutilated
as they were except by the
person criminally responsible
for the death—
desiring to conceal
evidence of his guilt.

If you are satisfied that the
persons whose remains were
found in that cellar
died of hyoscine poisoning

Who administered the poison ?

A drug not commonly known
to persons without
medical training
not commonly used even by
medical men.

PURCHASE OF HYOSCINE.

17/19 Jan. 1910. Crippen bought of Lewis & Burrows Ltd
5 grs Hyoscine Hydrobrom.

—500 to 1000 doses
Signed " Poisons Book."

He purported to do so on
Munyon's behalf for Homeopathic Preparations
which was untrue.

He had been a customer there for
about ten months and had never
bought hyoscine before.

What did he want it for ?
What did he do with it ?

Enormous quantity.
Lewis & Burrows had none
in stock.

Never in three years had near
that quantity in stock,

And then came three final dramatic questions :

What has become of Belle Elmore ?

Whose remains are those ?

If they are Belle Elmore's, what is the explanation of their being found in that place and in that mutilated condition ?

DR. CRIPPEN IN THE DOCK AT THE OLD BAILEY.

MISS PHYLLIS DARE.

Writers and stage performers loomed large among the spectators. And during one morning, the actress Phyllis Dare, recently dubbed 'The Belle of Mayfair', sat beside the judge, directly beneath the Sword of Justice.

"TRACKED BY WIRELESS."

Melodrama, in Five Acts, Adapted from *Answers* Serial "Blackmail," and Produced for the First Time at the Shakespeare Theatre, Clapham Junction, on Monday, Oct. 17.

The latest development in the art of tracking criminals is dramatised in the above-mentioned play, which had a hearty reception from a crowded house at the Shakespeare on Monday. Many thrilling situations are evolved in the course of the piece, which is, indeed, overburdened with incident, while the sympathetic interest of the piece is uncertain. There is, nevertheless, plenty of material attractive to the lovers of transpontine melodrama, and with judicious condensation the play should prove a valuable addition to the wares offered by the Melodrama Production Syndicate.

The characters are strongly drawn, and some resemblance is found to the chief figures of a notorious case at present engaging the courts. There is a City typist named Marion Rivers, who has been innocently involved in some shady transactions in a firm where she was employed, the head of which, Morton Wentmore, has in his possession letters written by Marion which would seem to prove her complicity in the frauds.

Excerpt from a leader, 'The Crippen Trial', in *The Times*, 24 October:

. . . The trial was all that it ought to be where life and death are at stake; with no hurry, no excitement, no introduction of disturbing elements – something of which Englishmen may be proud. Only one feature of the trial is to be regretted. It had some accessories which, it is to be hoped, will not attend future trials for murder, and against which, it is to be earnestly desired, Judges will set their faces. A Criminal Court is not a show room, nor is such a trial of the nature of a *matinée*; the Old Bailey is not a place to which fashionable ladies may fitly go in search of the latest sensation, where actors may hope to pick up suggestions as to a striking gesture or a novel expression, and where descriptive writers may look for good copy. All that a trial ought to be so far as the demeanour of those professionally concerned, this trial is a warning of the danger of an increase in accessories which are wholly inconsistent with the atmosphere of a Court of Justice; and it is to be hoped that in future there will be less readiness to gratify obtrusive and not altogether harmless curiosity.

THE END OF THE CRIPPEN TRIAL.

THE LORD CHIEF JUSTICE PASSING SENTENCE OF DEATH ON HAWLEY HARVEY CRIPPEN FOR THE MURDER OF HIS WIFE AT HILLDROP CRESCENT, AT THE CENTRAL CRIMINAL COURT ON SATURDAY.

According to Sir Richard Muir's biographers:

There has never been a murder case in which the accused person so clearly condemned himself as Crippen. Of course it was vitally necessary for him to go into the witness-box to deny the theories put forward by Muir. Had he not done so the jury would have found him guilty without leaving the box, but nevertheless by subjecting himself to Muir's deadly cross-examination he condemned himself out of his own mouth. A precisely similar occurrence took place in March, 1912, when Frederick Henry Seddon was on trial for his life, but whereas Seddon convicted himself as a cold-blooded, premeditated murderer by the self-possession he revealed under the cross-examination of Sir Rufus Isaacs, Crippen crumbled up and so contradicted himself that he stood revealed as a liar with an impossible story.

Although Crippen in his way was an able man possessed of an iron nerve, Muir wore him down until towards the end of the cross-examination his answers became wild and his guilt apparent even to those curiously minded persons who had failed to realize that the evidence for the prosecution was in truth irrefutable.

There is no necessity for me to recapitulate in full the grim story unfolded at the Old Bailey during the course of the trial. It will stand for all time as a unique example of forensic ability on the part of a Treasury Counsel. From the moment Muir took charge of the case he put in an almost incredible amount of work piecing together the long train of suspicious circumstances which were in evidence from the time of Mrs. Crippen's disappearance.

Weeks of arduous work, particularly that dealing with the medical evidence, had to be devoted to preparing the Crown brief. All the people associated with the case worked without cessation. They refused other work so that they might devote their attention to the conviction of Crippen. With Travers Humphreys, Ingleby Oddie and the detective officers concerned Muir worked on the case all hours of the night. There were endless consultations which also took place while the trial was actually in progress. After leaving the Old Bailey at night Muir would take his colleagues to his chambers in the Temple, where he would start off with a long list of topics for discussion neatly arranged on separate sheets of paper each with references to the page of the depositions and proofs, and underlined in various colours which he always used in making notes.

I suppose I am not divulging any great secret when I say that everybody connected with the prosecution of Crippen heartily cursed his name long before the trial concluded. Muir's consultations would begin shortly after the rising of the court. About half-past seven there would be a short interval for dinner, after which the topics would be resumed. In vain for the juniors and the medical men to suggest fatigue or the elimination of any matter as being of but slight importance. Muir would not have it. He would go solidly through the topics until they, like the consultants, were exhausted. He spared neither himself nor others in his conscientious determination to convict the accused man, thereby completely fulfilling the fears which Crippen expressed when his solicitor, Arthur Newton, brought him the news that the redoubtable R. D. Muir would conduct the prosecution for the Crown.

His cross-examination of Crippen will live for ever in the memory of the people who heard it. He began by asking the prisoner significant questions which practically determined his guilt from the very beginning.

" On the morning of February 1 you were left alone in your house with your wife ? " asked Muir quietly.

" Yes."

" She was alive ? "

" She was."

" And well ? " persisted Muir.

" She was."

" Do you know of any person in the world who has seen her alive since ? " asked Muir amid a tense silence.

" I do not."

" Do you know of any person in the world who has ever had a letter from her since ? "

" I do not."

" Do you know of any person in the world who can prove any fact showing that she ever left that house alive ? "

" Absolutely not. I have told Mr. Dew exactly all the facts."

Such answers in themselves, taken in conjunction with the damning facts already stated by the prosecution, were more than sufficient to have convicted Crippen, but Muir had no intention of allowing the prisoner to return to the dock until he had dragged from him what was practically a confession.

" Where did you think your wife had gone ? " asked Muir sternly, after he had put Crippen through a searching ordeal as to what had happened on the day (February 1) when his wife was supposed to have disappeared.

" I supposed," said Crippen, whose composure had not then deserted him, " that as she had always been talking about Bruce Miller to me, that she had gone there. That was the only thing I could make."

" That is to America ? "

" To America," said Crippen.

" Have you made inquiries ? " asked Muir.

" No."

" As to what steamers were going to America on or about that date ? " asked Muir determined to clear up that point.

" No, I have not," replied Crippen.

" At no time ? "

" At no time," said Crippen looking at Muir, wondering probably what damning question he would have to answer next.

" Not since your arrest ? "

" Not at all."

" What ! " exclaimed Muir, and as he did so he looked at the jury so that they should fully realize the importance of Crippen's admission when he said that not at any time had he made the slightest inquiry as to what had actually become of his wife.

There are some criminals who when under cross-examination are more than a match for opposing counsel, but it soon became evident that Crippen had neither the nerve nor the knowledge successfully to counteract the fatal impression of guilt which soon became established in the minds of every one listening to this sensational trial.

Muir extorted from the prisoner one admission after another, compelling him to confess that he had made no inquiries concerning any woman resembling his wife who might have travelled on a boat to America, that he had not even been to the cab stand at the bottom of Hilldrop Crescent to ascertain whether she might have taken a cab from there to remove her belongings, that he had not even inquired of the neighbours on either side to discover whether she had been seen leaving the house, nor had he even questioned the tradesmen who usually called with their food. In sober truth, an insignificant adversary for the greatest criminal lawyer in the land.

But Muir was fully determined to spare Crippen nothing, notwithstanding the guilt which slowly but surely revealed itself in every answer he made.

" On March 25," he said to Crippen, " you sent a telegram to Mrs. Martinetti, saying that you had received a cable that your wife had died the previous night ? "

" Yes," replied Crippen in a quiet voice which he had not raised once during the whole of his ordeal.

" You sent that from Victoria Station on the eve of your departure with Ethel Le Neve ? "

" Yes."

" On March 30, when you returned, Mrs. Martinetti and Mrs. Smythson came to see you about your wife's death ? "

" Yes."

" Were you in mourning ? " asked Muir, who did not intend to spare Crippen from the full revelation of his disgraceful hypocrisy.

" I could not say."

" Think," said Muir, looking straight at Crippen, " were you in mourning ? "

" I did put mourning on afterwards," replied Crippen, " but I could not say whether that day I had mourning clothes on or not."

In the subsequent question by the Lord Chief Justice he did admit that he had worn mourning afterwards. Muir took him through the whole gamut of his scandalous behaviour at that time, of how he had written to his wife's friends on black-edged paper, telling them of her death, and how he had nearly been out of his mind with the worry of it.

Crippen himself admitted it to be the sheerest hypocrisy and, when he realized how his answers were affecting the jury, he summoned up a show of indignation and said to Muir that he did not see why he should keep on with his questions, because he was willing to admit then and there that they were all lies from beginning to end. But whatever Crippen may have been, he was certainly one of the poorest liars who ever stood in the witness-box at the Old Bailey on a capital charge. So flagrant was the tale he sought to make the jury believe that ultimately he felt constrained to acknowledge that the explanation of his wife's absence which he had put about was nothing but a lie all through. Muir would not spare him one iota, but nevertheless Crippen, even after admitting that he had fabricated a mass of untruth, persisted in putting forward still another story in the hope that he might save his neck.

" For whose sake were you going through this elaborate process ? " asked Muir sarcastically.

" For the sake of both of us," said Crippen.

" What, for your sake ? " inquired Muir. " What did it matter to you ? "

" Well," said Crippen, " I did not wish the friends here to think I had treated her so badly that she had gone away and left me."

" You did not wish your friends here to think you had treated her badly ? "

" Yes."

" And going about, as you were, with Ethel Le Neve ? "

" That was not public," said Crippen.

" And how were you saving yourself from anything by telling those lies ? " asked Muir.

" I was saving myself from the scandal of my friends."

" Now," said Muir, " you treated your wife well ? "

" Yes."

" Given her money ? "

" Yes."

" And jewels ? "

" She had them to wear."

" And clothes ? "

" Yes."

" And kept up an establishment for her for four years after you had ceased to cohabit with her, when she treated you with ingratitude and went away and left you with no cause at all ? "

" Yes," said Crippen little recking the damage he was doing himself by his answers.

" But why should you seek to cover up a scandal for such a wife as that ? "

" I do not think I can explain it any further than I have."

Muir then proceeded to take the prisoner through that part of the story dealing with the finding of Mrs. Crippen's remains in the cellar of the house at Hilldrop Crescent. He elicited from him that he knew what had been found there, but that the remains must have been placed in the cellar without the knowledge of either himself or his wife, though he certainly condescended to say that such a thing was highly improbable. So Muir thereupon fired at him a few questions about the pyjamas which I have referred to in another part of this chapter, obtaining from him an admission that the jacket in which Mrs. Crippen's remains were buried must have been bought after the time when he went to live at Hilldrop Crescent, clearly indicating that the remains must have been buried in the cellar during the time of his tenancy. It is doubtful whether Crippen himself appreciated the significance of his answers, because, if the remains were definitely identified as being those of Mrs. Crippen, then the whole story of his defence amounted to a complete fabrication. So important was the matter that the Lord Chief Justice asked Crippen if he would like the opportunity of altering his reply. Muir put the question to the prisoner but he shook his head and said he did not.

And so it went on, with Muir extracting one deadly admission after another until Crippen's answers began to grow wild and it became plainly evident that his elaborate concoction of lies was engulfing him. Of course all the circumstances in this amazing passion of crime had contributed to the conviction of the accused man. His flight from London, the lies he had told to account for his wife's disappearance, so gravely prejudiced him that long before the trial was over his guilt was more or less a foregone conclusion.

In a good many ways Muir was extremely dissatisfied with the manner in which the police officers had carried out their work. He strongly criticized them for not arresting Crippen before he made his escape, pointing out that the suspicious circumstances which revealed themselves from the beginning of the time when Mrs. Crippen's disappearance was first reported necessitated infinitely stronger action than was actually taken.

Against this, it must be recollected that during the preliminary police inquiries with which he was faced before his flight Crippen showed an iron nerve and most astounding coolness, even when Chief-Inspector Walter Dew went down with him into the fatal cellar at Hilldrop Crescent to ascertain whether by any chance he could discover any trace of the missing woman. Perhaps it might be interesting if I gave Muir's own opinion of Crippen :

" He is not the ordinary type of man one would expect to commit a murder and then to cut up the body of his victim and dispose of it. Rather is he the sort of man I would expect to find running a successful swindle. He has a certain amount of craftiness and cunning, as well as considerable self-assurance.

" There is no doubt," added Muir, " that his life with his wife had been one of unending misery, and apparently he found a good deal of relief and a certain stolen happiness with Ethel Le Neve.

" I suppose one cannot look upon the cutting up of his wife's body as being such an outrageous or aggravating feature as it might have been with anyone else. He had more than a passing knowledge of medicine and surgery and to such a person, no doubt, the dissecting of a body would not create such a revolting impression as it would in an ordinary individual."

The case of Dr. Crippen will be notable for all time because of it being the first occasion on which a murderer poisoned his victim by means of that hitherto little-known drug hyoscine.

THE FOREMAN OF THE JURY ANNOUNCING THE VERDICT.

To Mr̄ R. D. Lowns & Son,
12 Ashbrook Grove, Upper Holloway

I authorize my Solicitor Mr Arthur Newton to sell the whole of my Furniture & Effects at 39 Hilldrop Crescent, & to pay the 2 quarters rents, which will become due on the 29ᵗʰ of September, & also the Gas Bill & Water Rate—

1. September 1910.

H.H.Crippen

CRIPPEN TO HANG.

CLOSING SCENES OF GREAT MURDER TRIAL.

THE DAILY GRAPHIC, MONDAY, OCTOBER 24, 1910.

CRIPPEN'S FATE.

NOTABLE TRIAL ENDS IN SENTENCE OF DEATH.

IMPRESSIVE SCENE.

Dr. Crippen was convicted of the murder of his wife, and sentenced to death at the Old Bailey on Saturday. Our special representative describes the scene in this column. Mr. Muir's address to the jury and the Lord Chief Justice's summing-up appear on page 10.

(BY OUR SPECIAL REPRESENTATIVE.)

It is seventeen minutes to three, and the jury have been absent for twenty-eight minutes. An usher enters carrying the terrible exhibits which have been examined by the jury in their retiring-room. So we know that the jury have considered their verdict and arrived at a decision. So we know that the fate of Dr. Crippen is settled, that the question of life or death has been decided for him in twenty-eight minutes! A surprise thrills through the crowded court because an indefinable rumour or belief had been flitting among us suggesting that the jury would have difficulty in agreeing, that perhaps one would prove obdurate and stand out against his fellows. And yet, remembering the summing-up of the Lord Chief Justice, so scrupulously fair and yet so remorselessly logical in its sequences of correlated facts and reasonable inferences, there was actually no reason for surprise. For each man in his heart had condemned the prisoner.

A pale, orange-tinted light floods the court as the jury stumble back into their places, is thrown downwards on the mass of tense, upturned faces from some crevices in the ceiling, and starts strange, fantastic shadows flickering in our midst. The judge, holding up a fold of his deep scarlet gown, enters slowly and resumes his seat.

"Are you agreed upon your verdict, gentlemen?" The foreman of the jury is about to reply, when the judge intervenes.

"We must have the prisoner here," says he.

CRIPPEN'S LAST APPEARANCE.

Yes, it is certainly essential that Dr. Crippen should be present! We hear a patter of light footsteps on the stairs leading up to the dock, and for the last time Dr. Crippen appears in that scene which must be now so familiar to him. He steps up briskly, disdaining the assistance of the banister. He has his black overcoat swung over one arm. He seems quite strong, self-dependent, and without constraint. But he has changed since we first saw him, changed since he stood smiling and chatting in the witness-box. He has grown older;

a look of age has come into his face. It is a parched face, dry and scribbled over and over with new sad lines. His eyes quiver no longer; they have grown steadfast. Always prominent, they now seem to actually bulge against the lenses of his bevelled spectacles. He looks straight at the jury, at each juryman, but it is not a look that could be construed by any flight of imagination into a glance of appeal; it is rather a keen scrutiny. He sits down, inscrutable, cold, self-possessed as ever. If there is a nerve aching in this extraordinary man's little body the only external sign is the twitch and contraction of his thin white hands.

A profound silence fills the court, silence and a sense of unusual doom. A clear, matter-of-fact, business-like voice breaks the silence, the Clerk of Arraigns repeating his question to the jury.

Yes, they are all agreed!

The foreman pauses, grips the ledge of the jury-box, and speaks huskily, with a slow utterance.

"We — find — the—prisoner—guilty—of—wilful—murder."

DOOMED.

Several women present cover their eyes. We hear a sob up in the gallery, where a white handkerchief flutters distinctly. The doomed man rises at a motion from a warder. His face is stained with a grey, leaden colour, and a little nerve works jumpily in his throat. But he finds no difficulty in rising. He even straightens himself into a more soldierly attitude than he has ever presented before. He looks straight before him, and if one can dare to read a definite suggestion in a man's looks at so supremely awful a moment, his hard blue eyes are hot with resentment.

Has he anything to say why sentence of death should not be pronounced upon him?

He pauses and clears his throat, which seems choked. At last he speaks, hoarsely, and in a low, guttural accent.

"I still protest my innocence."

The black cap is placed on the judge's head, and an usher calls through the silence for silence! The judge leans forward with his arms spread out upon the little table before him. He looks steadfastly at the prisoner, and in a strong, earnest voice pronounces the dread sentence of death. He will not dilate upon the ghastly and wicked nature of the crime, but he implores the doomed man to harbour no thoughts of a reprieve, but to make his peace with God.

"Amen."

The word is uttered by the silver-haired priest standing with bowed head near the judge's chair.

Dr. Crippen turns. The warders close in upon him, but he does not need their assistance. He walks steadily towards the stairway and passes for the last time from our sight, still impassive, still extremely calm, still inscrutable!

RANDAL CHARLTON.

LONDON MURDER MYSTERY.

Trial & Sentence

OF

Doctor H. H. CRIPPEN

For the Murder of

Belle Elmore (Mrs. Crippen),

Whose Mutilated Body was

Found in a Cellar in London.

THE NAUGHTY DOCTOR

A four-page leaflet that is being hawked around the town. A potted account of the case occupies the second page and the top of the third. The rest of the space is taken up by the following songs:

THE NAUGHTY DOCTOR

Tune: Yip-i-addy-i-ay.

We all know a man who done all he can
   To cause a sensation all round,
With fright we was filled, for they fancy he killed
   His dear wife and put her underground.
Then he hooked it away from us all one fine day,
   With his dear little typewriter too,
And they had a nice chase to find his sweet face,
   Soon right over the ocean he flew.

Chorus:

Crippen, my laddie, they'll make you pay,
   Whatever made you run away,
And pop off with your lover right over the sea,
   Dressed as a boy, and so smart was she.
Soon the piper you'll have to pay, hooray,
   They'll give you some physic one day,
At a end of a string, some day you might sing,
   Yip-i-addy-i-ay.

Now this artful gay feller he had a coal cellar.
   And we hear it was covered with bricks,
'Twas the scene of the crime if they'd bold him in time
   'Twould have put a stop to his tricks.
He smiled it appears, when he took 'em upstairs,
   And show'd 'em all over the house,
He bid 'em good-bye. Then next day done a guy
   With his donah as quiet as a mouse.

His escape, wild it made 'em, he tried to evade 'em,
   And bunked off from France into Spain,
In and out they both trott'd, his scheme was well
      plott'd,
   Too wide to come back again.
Then him and his Ethel, they boarded a vessel
   To bunk off to Canada's shore,
But somebody sold him, the captain he bold him,
   To send him to England once more.

JAMES LAURI

HE LEFT YOU FOR ANOTHER

(AIR: Nelly Dean.)

The world now mourns the loss of one so dear,
   Beloved by all her friends both far and near,
Her life's been took away, in a most inhuman way,
   The crime has caused a feeling sad and drear.
A loving wife she'd been to him for years,
   In silence yet no doubt shed bitter tears,
His heart to her grew cold and her grief remains untold
   Then to the world's surprise, poor Cora disappears.

Chorus:

He left you for another, Cora dear,
   He took your life for her, Cora dear,
In your grave now you lay low,
   He'll be punished as we know,
For the harm he did to you, my Cora dear.

We recall the day we missed you, Cora dear,
   Bid you good-night and kissed you, Cora dear,
Then at the break of morn, we found that you had
      gone
   We wondered what caused you to disappear.
Your husband he betrayed you, Cora dear,
   He killed you for another, Cora dear,
You're sleeping now on high, our hearts still heave a
      sigh,
   For those happy days gone by, Cora dear,

We all know his wicked motive, Cora dear,
   Belied by him you loved so, Cora dear,
But another came that way and he was tempted to
      slay
   The wife he should have loved, his Cora dear.
On yonder shore you're sleeping, Cora dear,
   All the angels watch they're keeping, Cora dear,
Poor darling, you've been slain, we'll in heaven meet
      again
   He'll be punished for his crime, Cora dear.

JAMES LAURI

SENTENCE ON DR. CRIPPEN

Tune: Please Mr. Conductor

'Twas London's Old Bailey and so crowded is the
   court,
   Excitement is stamped on each face,
There's Lords of the Land and Ladies so grand,
   To hear a sensational case.
The jury is sworn and silence is called,
   And the great Lord Chief Justice comes in,
Then the prisoner appears and the charge is read out,
   And the trial of Crippen begins.
Then Counsel stands up the jury to tell
   Of a cruel and a foul fiendish deed,
And our blood it runs cold as the story is told,
   Yet Crippen "not guilty" did plead.

Chorus:

But guilty was the verdict, Crippen he had been
   doomed
   He must die on the scaffold and lie in a murderer's
   tomb,
Short is the time for Repentance, let him for forgiveness implore,
   For sentenced has been Dr. Crippen for the murder
   of poor Belle Elmore.

The case for the Crown it grimly is told,
   And tears they dim every eye,
As the Counsel he told of the terrible way
   Poor Belle Elmore did die.
First poison is given and when it's done its work,
   The body, heartrending to say,
Was cruelly cut up in the dead of the night,
   And secretly hidden away.
While friends they were searching for her everywhere,
   Their searching was of no avail,
In Hilldrop Crescent the murdered did lie,
   But Justice was soon on the trail.

Then for the defence in grand eloquence.
   Counsel he, Crippen defends,
And the prisoner is called and the Court is enthralled,
   So much on his statement depends.
But soon it is o'er and the Judge he sums up,
   And the jury their verdict return,
They found Crippen guilty of murder so foul,
   Then the Judge speaks in tones sad but stern.
Harvey Hawley Crippen you've guilty been found
   Of a murder most fiendishly done,
For which you must die, and to God on High,
   Pray for mercy, for here, there is none.

H. POULSON

CRIPPEN ADIEU

(AIR: Top o' the Morning.)

Poor old Crippen oh, he'll soon go below,
   Poking the fire and telling the tale,
The ladies loved him so, mad they're sure to go,
   For his loss they'll weep and wail.
You've been so naughty to kill your darling wife,
   All through this you lose your life, life,
What will Ethel do, she said she'd be true,
   You naughty boy to cause this strife.

Chorus:

Early one morning we'll bid him adieu,
   Dear Mr. Bogey he's waiting for you.
For miles, and miles and miles, over hills, and dales
   and stiles,
   All round the fire they're calling I've got room for
   you,
The ladies who love him, what will they do.
   Old mother Dyer she's asking for you,
So let's all pipe our eye, heave a sigh and say
   good-bye
   How do'ye do, top o' the morn, Crippen adieu!

With his typewriter he sailed across the sea,
   There he thought he wouldn't be seen,
Happy blithe and gay, he passed his time away
   Along with his tart, his dear little queen.
But now it is all over, he must bid us all good-bye,
   And leave his dear little cuddle behind, my
How they'll welcome him, give him cake and gin,
   When you're down there you'll never die.

When he's down below, won't he have a go,
   There's plenty of girls, he can do as he likes,
Kiss or cuddle 'em, poison or murder 'em,
   For exercise, there's plenty of bikes,
Then his Satanic Majesty will take him by the hand
   We want a doctor here so bad, and
Now you've come this way, please don't run away,
   Be enjoying yourself and doing the grand.

JAMES LAURI

THE NEW YORK TIMES,
OCTOBER 26, 1910.

MISS LENEVE FREED AFTER QUICK TRIAL

Jury Finds Her Not Guilty of Being Accessory After the Fact in Crippen Murder.

SUMMING UP IN HER FAVOR

Lord Alverstone Says He Sees No Reason Why Crippen Should Have Told the Girl of the Crime.

LONDON, Oct. 25.—After a trial lasting a few hours in the Old Bailey to-day a jury found Ethel Clara Leneve not guilty as an accessory after the fact in the murder of Cora Belle Crippen, for whose death her husband, Dr. Crippen, is to be hanged on Nov. 8.

Miss Leneve was in love with Dr. Crippen and slept in his house on the night of the day following that on which the doctor is supposed to have murdered his wife. She accompanied Crippen in his flight to Canada, and with him was arrested and indicted.

From the first she has maintained innocence of any knowledge of the crime, but the Crown alleged that her behavior subsequent to the disappearance of Mrs. Crippen, or Belle Elmore, as she was known on the stage, was such as to betray a guilty knowledge of the murder.

When arraigned to-day Miss Leneve pleaded " Not guilty." Witnesses were introduced by the prosecution to show that she had experienced periods of great mental distress after Belle Elmore's death. The Crown Prosecutor, Richard Muir, K. C., introduced only such evidence as had been brought out in the earlier hearings.

Miss Leneve's counsel, Frederick E. Smith, M. P., K. C., asked the jury to bear in mind that his client had been for years under the influence of Crippen, one of the most dangerous criminals of recent years. This, he asserted, accounted for her flight in the doctor's company. There was no proof, he declared, that she had guilty knowledge of the crime. He said he took upon his own shoulders the responsibility for not putting Miss Leneve in the witness box.

Lord Chief Justice Alverstone, who presided, in summing up, said he saw no reason why Dr. Crippen should have told Miss Leneve a story different from that which he told to others.

As upon the occasion of Crippen's trial, the courtroom was to-day crowded with members of the legal profession and as many others as could obtain places by right or influence. There was, however, this difference: if Crippen had any well-wishers they kept in the background, while there was a noticeable sentiment of sympathy for the girl who, for love of a man nearly twice her age, had sacrificed her reputation, deserted home and friends, and remained true to him even when their association made her liable as an accessory to a brutal murder.

As Miss Leneve sat in the prisoner's dock she was a pathetic figure. She is 27 years of age, of medium build, with light brown hair, gray eyes, and excellent teeth. Her face is pretty and she is trim. She wears good clothes becomingly. To-day she was attired in the same neat blue costume which she wore at the preliminary hearing in the police court. She entered the dock between the wardresses and remained standing during the few minutes occupied by the swearing in of the jury.

Miss Leneve was an object of keen scrutiny on the part of the women, who composed the majority of the spectators. In reply to the formal charge of being accessory after the fact to the murder of Belle Elmore, the girl pleaded " not guilty " in a voice that was scarcely audible.

The Lord Chief Justice then called Mr. Muir, who outlined the case against the accused. It was clear, Mr. Muir said, that the intrigue between Crippen and Miss Leneve constituted the motive for the murder of Crippen's wife. He particularly dwelt upon the evidence given by Mrs. Jackson, Miss Leneve's landlady, at the preliminary hearing. The illness of the accused on the night of her interview with Mrs. Jackson was not, the Crown Prosecutor said, an ordinary illness, but a condition of horror, the explanation of which was the knowledge that had come to her that Crippen had murdered his wife.

Inspector Dew of Scotland Yard and the other witnesses for the Crown were taken rapidly through the evidence which they had given in the lower courts. No new testimony was brought out, and the prosecution closed its case before luncheon. Afterward Mr. Smith delivered his argument, Lord Alverstone summed up, and the jury quickly returned the verdict of not guilty.

Pentonville Prison
Friday, October 28, 1910

You can imagine what my feelings are to have before me your dear handwriting again. I have longed so passionately for a letter from you to sustain me through the long and weary separation, and, although I have been able to subdue my nerves and preserve my outward control, my heart has been bursting and throbbing with the pain of longing for you and even for a few written words from my ever-loving darling. I knew my darling's heart and love for me would never waver in the slightest, and hope sustained me, and that our union has not only been for life but for all eternity . . . .

I do not of course know if you are keeping your own name where you are staying, but I strongly advise you not to do so, and, wifie dear, it would please me so much if you would take my first name or my second Christian name, which you prefer — probably you prefer Hawley — and add 'Mrs' to it, as you will wear my (or our) ring as before. So tell me in your next how and where to address you, which will save delay.

My good things all came at once to-day. Your visit was a surprise. I have just returned from it, and sat down to my letter again. I nearly broke down, but struggled to be composed and not upset you. My own dear heart, how I longed even to touch your hand. To hold you in my arms would have been paradise, but we must look forward to that . . . .

Pentonville Prison
Tuesday, November 1, 1910

Your visit last evening was precious indeed to me, but I am afraid I did all the talking, darling, and you had no time to explain much. Probably you did not have time to write to me last night, as I have had no letter yet. Perhaps it may come later when the Governor comes in to see me.

In the meantime, wifie, I must content myself with those you have sent me up to now — four of them, and all treasured more than diamonds. I read them over and over again, and get great comfort from your loving words and the thought that, though we are separated, your love is all mine for always, as my love is yours to eternity. It is so precious a thought to me to tell you are always and ever my wifie, and that not even death can come between us. My heart rejoices in the promise that you will always bear the name you have taken, no matter what comes . . . .

Ethel in boy's clothes

5 November 1910

Seymour Hicks was at Bow Street Police Station, seeing a detective-friend, on the day of Crippen's appeal. 'Ethel Le Neve was in here a moment ago,' the detective told Hicks. 'She came in to know if she could borrow the pair of trousers she wore when she was arrested on board ship disguised as a boy.' The reason for the request, the detective explained, was that she had been offered a sum of money by a newspaper for being photographed in her runaway costume. 'While I was discussing the matter with her, the news came through that Crippen's appeal had failed and that he was to hang. The only comment she made was "Oh!"'

Lloyd's Weekly News, 20 November 1910:

Pentonville Prison
Saturday, November 5, 1910

The Appeal has decided against us. Hope has completely gone, and your hub's heart is broken. No more can he hold his wifie in his arms and the life he planned to devote to making your life comfortable is rapidly drawing to its end.

Death has no terror for me. I fear not at all the passing from this life, but, oh! wifie, my love, my own, the bitterness of the thought that I must leave you alone, without me in the world, to those who can never, I am sure, love you, cherish you, and protect you as I would have done hereafter as in the past . . . .

I shall feel bereft of everything indeed if I cannot give you at least one good-bye kiss, but oh! wifie dear, I am fearful it may not be permitted. Still, when I know what day our last farewell must be, I shall beg the Home Office to grant us that favour.

It is comfort to my anguished heart to know you will always keep my image in your heart, and believe, my darling, we *shall* meet again in another life. We have been always so entirely one in heart and soul, thought and deed, even in flesh and spirit, I cannot believe otherwise but that we shall be together in that other life I am going to soon.

I am not so selfish, darling, as wish you not to marry again, but inasmuch as you have been the one woman who has had all my heart, so do I believe you will ever keep me in your heart.

If only I could have left you well provided for I would have wished our little one had lived that you might have had what would have been part of both of us. But, like other things, it was not to be . . . .

If you can I should like to know your plans for the future before I am gone; it would be a comfort to me indeed to know how wifie, my own darling, is to be provided for . . . .

I have not been able to keep the tears back tonight, the bitter news of the disappointment has been so terrible, and my longings for my wifie have been so intense. But I shall soon be brave again and keep up to the end.

Were it possible I would wish to be *cremated*, and wish wifie then *to dispose of my ashes as she desires*. Please, darling, when you think of something to suggest or ask me, put it down on a memo, to write me about or to ask me when you see me. The time is short, and we must try and think of everything for wifie's benefit and get all settled for you that I can accomplish . . . .

Pentonville Prison
Sunday, November 6, 1910

One Sunday, how early I came for you — six years ago last summer it was — and we had a whole day together, which meant so much to us then. A rainy day indeed, but how happy we were together, with all sunshine in our hearts. It is good to think, darling wifie, that even in those early days before our wedding came that we were always in perfect harmony with each other. Even without being wedded.

Then came those days when hub felt, and wifie too so earnestly felt, it was impossible to live on and not be all in all to each other, and from our wedding day all has been a perfect honeymoon of four years to Dec. 6 next.

CRIPPEN'S FATHER DIES.

Was Penniless Through Lack of Remittances from Doctor, His Only Support.

LOS ANGELES, Cal., Nov. 18.—Myron H. Crippen, aged 88 years, father of Dr. Hawley H. Crippen, under sentence of death in London for the murder of his wife, died to-day in this city, friendless and penniless. His death, due to the infirmities of age, was hastened by grief over his son's crime.

Death occurred in a rooming house, and the only person at the aged man's bedside was the woman who managed the place. Hawley Crippen, a son of Dr. Crippen, was with his grandfather during the night, but left before death came.

Dr. Crippen was the sole support of his aged father. No remittance had come since the son's flight from London with Ethel Leneve and his arrest in Canada some months ago.

Facing actual starvation he was helped by a few persons whom he had come to know during his residence in Los Angeles. The rooming house kept him rent free, and a restaurant keeper, at whose place he had been accustomed to buy his meals, continued to supply them.

Chelsea, S.W.
November 22nd, 1910

Dear Mr Newton, – To-day, of course, I had my last interview with the man I loved so well and who is indeed dear to me. I do indeed pray that God will prove his innocence of the crime for which he was convicted and which I do not, neither do I consider he, knew anything about.

May God keep us both at this hour and bring us together in eternity is the wish of the woman who loves him, and who would, had she been able to, clear his name before the end. God, however, wills it, but I pray that He will assist my efforts in proving to the world his innocence, so that I can go to him with my duty fulfilled.

To-day he wrote to you telling you of the new will which he has made and which seems to give him so much comfort . . . .

With every good wish for your prosperity and happiness in the future, I am, Yours very sincerely.

ETHEL LE NEVE

Pentonville Prison
Monday, November 21, 1910

How can I find the strength and heart to struggle through this last letter? God, indeed, must hear our cry to Him for Divine help in this last farewell.

How to control myself to write I hardly know, but pray God help us to be brave to face the end now so near.

The thoughts rush to my mind quicker than I can put them down. Time is so short now, and there is so much that I would say.

There are less than two days left to us, only one more after this can I write you, and only two more visits, one before you read this letter and one to-morrow . . . .

Pentonville Prison
Tuesday, November 22, 1910

When I received your letter on Sunday eve I saw that you did not then know the bad news and I prayed God to help you in the morning when you did learn it.

I know what your agony will be, for I know your heart, like mine, will be broken. God help us indeed to be brave.

That is my constant prayer, now that the last refuge to which we had looked with some hope has fled.

I am comforted at least in thinking that throughout all the years of our friendship never have I passed one unkind word or given one reproachful look to her whom I have loved best in life, to whom I have given myself heart and soul, wholly and entirely for ever . . . .

Crippen's "Farewell Letter to the World",
published by several newspapers on about 20 November
"About my unhappy relations with Belle Elmore I will say nothing. We drifted apart in sympathy; she had her own friends and pleasures, and I was rather a lonely man and rather miserable. Then I obtained the affection and sympathy of Miss Le Neve. I confess that, according to the moral laws of Church and State, we were guilty, and I do not defend our position in that respect. But what I do say is that this love was not of a debased and degraded character. It was — if I may say so to people who will not perhaps understand or believe — a good love. She comforted me in my melancholy condition; her mind was beautiful to me; her loyalty and courage and self-sacrifice were of a high character. Whatever sin there was — and we broke the law — it was my sin, not hers . . . .

"In this farewell letter to the world, written as I face eternity, I say that Ethel Le Neve has loved me as few women love men, and that her innocence of any crime, save that of yielding to the dictates of the heart, is absolute. To her I pay this last tribute. It is of her that my last thoughts have been. My last prayer will be that God may protect her and keep her safe from harm, and allow her to join me in eternity.

"Surely such love as hers for me will be rewarded. However vile I am, whatever faults I may have committed, surely a woman whose love has been beyond all womanly loyalty, who though the world has condemned me believes in my innocence; who, though I am scorned by men, holds true to her love and is faithful to the last, has a virtue of love which may not be denounced by men who have not been so happy as I have been, or by women whose hearts are not big enough for such devotion. Remember that she has faced the agonies and tortures of being charged with murder, of enduring a long imprisonment, of facing a terrible prosecution before her acquittal. Yet she still loves me. Never once has she turned against me for all that unwillingly I have made her bear. Is not that a wonderful woman's love?

"Facing my Maker, very close to the hour of my death, I give my testimony to the absolute innocence of Ethel Le Neve. She put her trust in me, and what I asked her to do she did, never doubting. When I asked her to fly with me because of the scandal that would follow the discovery of Belle Elmore's disappearance, she believed the words I spoke, and said she would go with me and face whatever discomforts might follow. When I suggested the boy's disguise she adopted it with a girlish sense of amusement over which there was no shadow of guilt. Poor child! Why should she feel guilty? She had been overwhelmed with surprise to hear that Belle Elmore was still alive. But she had forgotten my first and only deception — the story of the cablegrams announcing Belle Elmore's death.

"Her only idea was that we were getting away to a new world and a new life, away from prying eyes and gossiping tongues. She was willing to adventure all for that, and she still trusted me. I believe she has told in full detail the story of her adventures in boy's clothes, and although I have not been permitted to read a line of her narrative, I know that every word is true, for she has the heart of truth. I feel sure also that she has said no unkind word about me . . . .

"I make this defence and this acknowledgment — that the love of Ethel Le Neve has been the best thing in my life — my only happiness — and that in return for that great gift I have been inspired with a greater kindness towards my fellow-beings, and with a greater desire to do good. We were as man and wife together, with an absolute communion of spirit. Perhaps God will pardon us because we were like two children in the great unkind world, who clung to one another and gave each other courage.

"In Rotterdam and Brussels, and during the voyage across the Atlantic on the 'Montrose', Ethel had no suspicion of the tragedy that awaited her. Always she was hopeful of the future and full of expectation of the adventures to come. Then as a bolt from the blue came the arrival of Inspector Dew, with the appalling charges made against us both, followed by our dreadful separation.

"The world knows what happened afterwards; but what it does not know is the agony we both suffered, the frightful torture of two hearts beating one for another, yet divided by the most cruel barriers."

Extracts apropos of Crippen from the 1910 diary of the Governor of Pentonville Prison

Oct. 23 Complains of the cold. Slept well and says he is not a bit worried.

Nov. 3 Is not so cheerful to-day and says he feels his nerves are inclined to give way a bit after the long strain. Did not sleep at all well last night.

Nov. 4 Says he cannot sleep and the only thing that does him any good under the circumstances is stout. Recommended that the above be trimmed about the face where required with "Clippers" and that scissors or razors or any other instrument should not be used.

Nov. 10 Sleeps all right. Says he enjoys his steak immensely.

Nov. 19 No reprieve.

Nov. 20 Very careworn and pale.

Nov. 21 Broke off rim of glass whilst retiring to lavatory with the presumed idea of attempting self-injury.

Nov. 23 Execution 9 a.m.

A print – presumably intended to be framed for hanging – that is being retailed. The artist's imagination has overstepped the bounds of verisimilitude. Who on earth is the gentleman in the wig? Are we to suppose that Mr Ellis, the usually cloth-capped executioner, has, specially for the big death-dealing moment of his life, patronized Messrs. Moss Brothers' formal-dress hire department? . . . and purchased a beard from Willie Clarkson?

A reliable outline of the executional procedure is provided by Gilbert Hair, governor of several prisons during his career, in a letter – written in confidence, of course – to his friend, the writer, Miss F. Tennyson Jesse:

On reception on remand, a murderer is weighed, etc. On reception on conviction, he goes straight to the condemned cell and not the reception ward. In the cell he is changed into prison clothes, etc., and very carefully searched. The same day papers are sent to a large number of people who have to carry out the execution formalities – Sheriff, Secretary of State, etc., etc.

Two weeks before the execution, the rope, cap, wire, chalk, string, etc. are tested on the drop with a bag of sand which is the same weight as the prisoner.

The day before an execution, the executioner and his assistant have to be in the prison by 4 p.m. They are not allowed outside the gates again till after the execution. We give them beds, food, and "two pints of malt liquor" each if they want it.

Condemned men usually exercise about 6-7 p.m., and opportunity is given for the executioner to see the prisoners during the evening to get an idea of his build, neck, etc. The prisoner never sees him.

The drop is prepared the night before, while the man is at exercise.

On the morning of an execution, the man wakes up to find his prison clothes gone, and the clothes he was tried in waiting for him – less collar and tie. That is the worst moment of all.

Two officers have been with the man day and night for three weeks (three Sundays must elapse between sentence and death). The night men are relieved at 7 a.m. and the men who are going to the drop with the prisoner come on duty then.

Half an hour before the execution, the Chaplain usually goes into the cell, after the man has had breakfast, and stays there till five to the hour.

The amount of brandy issued is the amount you get in a double brandy in an hotel, and it is invariably accepted by the prisoner a few minutes before he is executed.

On the stroke of the hour, the door of the condemned cell opens to admit the executioners. The senior pinions the man, they turn, and, preceded by the Chaplain, walk to the drop. Officers 1 and 2 on plan come with the man from the condemned cell and stand on boards to support him if necessary. The second the prisoner is on the chalked square (hence the chalk), the second hangman pinions his legs, stands clear – and he's dead.

As you will see by my plan, the prisoner, Chaplain, etc., pass the Sheriff, Governor, etc., in the ante-room of the execution shed. Usually the Sheriff is well in the rear, and unless you are in front and quick you don't see anything at all of the drop.

You see, the only people in the condemned cell are the prisoner and his two officers, the Chaplain, and the executioner. We wait in the ante-room. As soon as he drops, the doctor goes down and tests his heart. Then he comes up and signs death certificates, etc.

The man is left hanging in the locked shed for an hour, then taken to the mortuary for post-mortem and inquest. An hour later, he is buried and his clothes burnt.

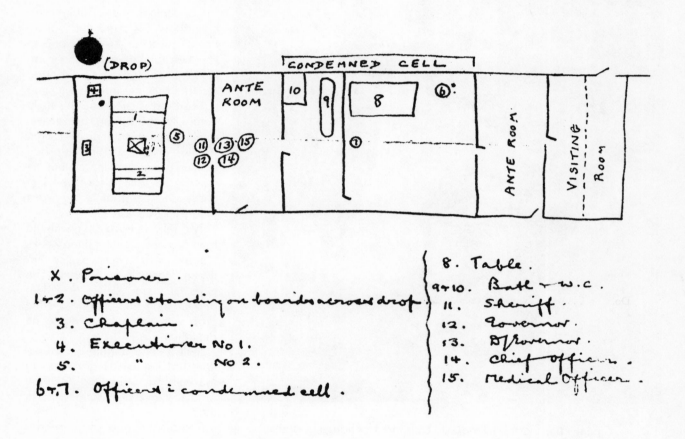

X . Prisoner.

1 + 2 . Officers standing on boards across drop.

3 . Chaplain .

4 . Executioner No 1.

5 .   "   No 2 .

6 + 7 . Officers i condemned cell .

8 . Table .

9 + 10 . Bath + w.c.

11 . Sheriff .

12 . Governor .

13 . D/Governor .

14 . Chief Officer .

15 . Medical Officer .

Notes made by the Governor of Pentonville Prison on an index-card headed "CRIPPEN, H.H.":

Wt. on reception, remand	136 lb.	
on admission, guilty	142 lb.	
Ht.	5' 4"	
Drop	7' 9"	

No stretching of rope.

Fracture of vertebral column high up about 3rd cervical vertebrae.

Fell dead – 60 seconds.

The Times, 23 November

OUTWARD-BOUND STEAMERS
FROM NOVEMBER 23RD TO 29TH INCLUSIVE
Compiled from the Advertisements in **The Times** *Shipping Columns, which should be consulted for details:—*

Destination	Line	Leaves	
Argen. & S. Amer.	R.M.S.P.	S'ton & C'g	Nov. 25
Australia, &c.	P. and O.	Mars'les,	Nov. 25
Do.	Orient	London,	Nov. 25
Do.	British India	London,	Nov. 23
Do.	N.D.L.	S'th'ton,	Nov. 28
Bombay, &c.	P. and O.	London,	Nov. 25
Boston	White Star	Liverp'l,	Nov. 29
Calcutta, &c.	P. and O.	London,	Nov. 26
Do.	Harrison	Liverp'l,	Nov. 25
Do.	Brocklebank	Liverp'l,	Nov. 25
Canada	White Star	Liverp'l,	Nov. 24
Egypt	Austrian-Lloyd	Trieste,	Nov. 24
Do., Cey., Burma	Bibby	Mars'les,	Nov. 25
Mahé, &c.	M.M.	Mars'les,	Nov. 25
Natal, &c.	Aberdeen	London,	Nov. 29
New York	Cunard	Liverp'l,	Nov. 26
Do. (S.S. Majestic)	White Star	S'th'ton,	Nov. 23
Do.	Do.	Liverp'l,	Nov. 26
Do.	American	S'th'ton,	Nov. 26
Do.	A.T.L.	London,	Nov. 24
Do.	Hamburg-Amer	S'th'ton,	Nov. 27
Do.	Anchor	Glasgow,	Nov. 26
New Zealand, &c.	N.Z. Ship Co.	London,	Nov. 24
South Africa	Union-Castle	London,	Nov. 25
Do.	Do.	S'th'ton,	Nov. 26
South America	Pacific	Liverp'l,	Nov. 25
Straits, China, &c.	Austrian-Lloyd	Trieste,	Nov. 27
Do.	Nippon Yusen	London,	Nov. 26

JOHN BULL.
DECEMBER 17TH, 1910.

One of the greatest mistakes Crippen ever made in his life was in not avoiding his " key numbers." According to Cheiro, the amazing gentleman who can see through a brick wall as far as most people, if not farther, Crippen's key numbers were fours and eights; so that, if he had only stuck to fives and nines he might have been a respected, honoured, and unhanged citizen. It was his obvious duty to avoid the year he was born in, '62, for 6 and 2 are 8; likewise, he should have stayed away from that dinner with the Martinetti's on January 31st, for 3 and 1 make 4. He made his statement to Inspector Dew on July 8, and then, to make things worse, he lets Dew find the remains in the cellar on July 13th, for again 3 and 1 are 4. Then the foolish man called himself " Robinson," a name of eight letters, when he might just as well have travelled as Brown or Smith. Not only so, but he sails in the *Montrose*, again a name of eight letters; comes back in the *Megantic* for trial, eight letters again; and, worst blunder of all, he allowed his key numbers to come together in the year he was hanged, being 48 years old when he was executed. We hope there is nobody living with key numbers like Crippen's, unless it is Lord Lansdowne, Mr. Asquith, Mr. Balfour, Mr. Lloyd George, Mr. John Redmond, Mr. Churchill, and Mr. F. E. Smith; then in due course we shall probably get a little peace. So will they.

CRIPPEN HANGED TO-DAY AT PENTONVILLE

HOW HE MURDERED BELLE ELMORE AND MADE AWAY WITH
THE BODY

HIS FULL CONFESSION

THE POISON WAS ADMINISTERED IN INDIGESTION TABLETS

The above were the front-page headlines of this day's editions of a new London paper, the *Evening Times*, whose circulation had never exceeded 100,000. Today, the presses ran almost without pause, churning out nigh on a million copies.

The explanation given for the confession's being in the third person was that "Dr Crippen, before he died, confessed his guilt to a friend who has, unable to hold his awful secret any longer, given the full facts to the 'Evening Times'". The writer of the introduction asserted: "It is a story which speaks for itself, and is, perhaps, one of the most remarkable and thrilling narratives which all the annals of crime can furnish." But, actually, it was neither remarkable nor thrilling. What the "confession" boiled down to was that Crippen had poisoned his wife by administering hyoscine in indigestion tablets made by Munyon's, and had cut up her body with a surgeon's knife, which he had subsequently hidden in the garden of an empty house in Hilldrop Crescent.

The story behind the story is told in, among other volumes, Margaret Lane's biography of Edgar Wallace, who in 1910 was racing editor of the *Evening Times*. A few days before the execution, a man called at the offices of the newspaper and confided to the editor, Charles Watney, that Crippen had made a confession to his solicitor, Arthur Newton — who was prepared to sell it for £1,000. A meeting was arranged between Newton and the paper's advertising manager, Arthur Findon. Newton accepted an offer of £500, saying that he would dictate a statement from notes, on the understanding that his name would not be connected with the story. At a later meeting, the fee was paid to Newton (in gold sovereigns, as he had stipulated), and he promised to dictate the story on the eve of the execution. After the *Evening Times* had put out posters announcing the confession, Newton, frightened that the Law Society had got wind of the arrangement, said that he was going back on his promise — whereupon Charles Watney threatened to publish an account of the aborted deal.

"Terrified now by the possible professional consequences to himself, whichever way he acted, Newton finally in the small hours of the morning promised to dictate the confession to a friend, who in turn undertook to deliver it at Arthur Findon's flat within a few hours. Accordingly, at about three o'clock on the morning of the execution, the anonymous friend arrived with the written narrative, which he refused to allow out of his hands; he would dictate it, he said, and then only on the understanding that Newton was not to be quoted as an authority, and that the original document was to be burned as soon as ready. Findon and another member of the *Evening Times* staff took it down from his dictation, and in some anguish watched him throw the original copy on the fire. The partially burned remains of it they rescued as soon as he had gone, to serve as some sort of evidence of the authenticity of the confession.

"At five o'clock on the morning of the 23rd the confession was in the office, where most of the editorial staff, including Edgar Wallace, were anxiously expecting it . . . . Edgar (who had nursed a particular affection for the murderer since learning from Captain Kendall's statement that Crippen, during the Atlantic crossing which had ended in his arrest, had been 'busy reading *The Four Just Men* [by Wallace], which is all about a murder') was told by Charles Watney to improve it still further with 'half a column of good human intro'."

Part of the intro has already been quoted. Another part read: "The statement printed below is Crippen's own statement. It bears in every line the stamp of authenticity. It is unnecessary to say that no journal — even the least responsible of journals — would print this confession of Crippen's without unimpeachable authority. That authority we possess."

Margaret Lane goes on to say that, following the appearance of the first edition of the *Evening Times*, "the other newspapers had not been idle; they had applied both to Newton and to the governor and warders of Pentonville for confirmation of the 'confession', and had received emphatic and official denials from all of them. The *Evening News* and *Star* flooded the streets with bills announcing: 'CRIPPEN: NO CONFESSION', and the *Evening Times*, when challenged to produce its proofs, was miserably dumb. [Newton: 'It is not within any man's right to throw doubt on the confession. So far as I personally am concerned, I can say nothing about the confession. I personally knew of no confession, and beyond this I cannot discuss the matter.'] For want of any better support, the *Evening Times* was thoroughly discredited, and by the next day its sales had dropped ominously to 60,000. The solicitor consulted unhesitatingly advised the directors to publish the whole story, making clear Newton's part in the affair . . . but Sir Samuel Scott, one of the Members of Parliament financing the paper, was against taking such a step, it being his opinion that while the *Evening Times* would eventually live the matter down, such an exposure would inevitably ruin Newton."

Within a few months, the *Evening Times* was dead. Though Arthur Newton escaped retribution in regard to the "confession", he was less fortunate apropos of deals with other journals, particularly *John Bull*:

Early in 1911, the Committee of the Law Society found that Newton "had on November 21, 1910, in the capacity of legal adviser to one Crippen, been permitted to visit him when a convict detained in his Majesty's prison, Pentonville, under sentence of death, and, in abuse of the privilege thus extended to him, aided and abetted one Horatio Bottomley, the editor of *John Bull*, to disseminate in that publication false information in the form of a letter purporting to have been written by Crippen from prison, although, as the respondent well knew, no such letter in fact existed, and had further published or permitted to be published through the medium of *John Bull* and the *Daily Chronicle* other false statements relating to the same matter, well knowing them to be false, whereby the public might be deceived, and the Committee reported that the respondent had been guilty of professional misconduct within the meaning of the Solicitors Act, 1888."

On 12 July 1911, the King's Bench Division of the High Court ordered that "Arthur Newton, of 23 Great Marlborough Street, solicitor, be suspended for 12 months from 25 July 1911, and that he pay the costs of the inquiry and of the hearing".

(Almost exactly two years later, Newton was sentenced to three years' penal servitude for defrauding an Austrian businessman and for converting property entrusted to him; consequently, the Law Society ordered that he be struck from the rolls as a solicitor. Upon his release from Parkhurst Prison, he became a private investigator, and developed a sideline as a marriage-broker between impoverished aristocrats and *nouveaux riches*. He died on 3 October 1930.)

NOVEMBER 26TH, 1910.   JOHN BULL.   829

CRIPPEN'S REPLY TO OUR LETTER.

HE DECLINES TO IMPLICATE OTHERS AND IS CONCERNED ONLY FOR MISS LE NEVE'S FUTURE—BUT HINTS AT POSSIBLE REVELATIONS.

Our readers will remember that last week we addressed the following letter to Crippen :—

HARVEY HAWLEY CRIPPEN,—The days are rapidly passing, and every sunrise brings you nearer to that grim morning when you will hear the solemn announcement that your time has come. Heaven forbid that I should say a word to intensify the mental anguish which, in the meantime, you must be enduring. Were you as vile and black as the verdict of that jury has declared you—were you just that cold and callous murderer which the Law has proclaimed you to be—even then, I would ask you to let me extend to you the hand of a brother. I would talk no clap-trap about Forgiveness and Repentance—I would picture to you no Paradise of the Blessed, bidding you to enter. I would just say, "Brother, how came you to do it? What demon possessed you? Relieve your burning brain by confiding all to me." And I would ask you to go upon your knees and pray to *her* to forgive you. All said, she was a woman, you know, and if beyond what we call Death there be a Life, she would hear your prayer—and who knows that she would not, of that wondrous mystery of a woman's soul, say "I forgive"? In any case, Crippen, it were worth the doing—and you would be a better, and a stronger, man for doing it.

But it is not to speak thus to you that I am writing. I have something else to say—something which is weighing heavily upon me. A man of many activities, in close touch with human affairs, much comes to me—some of it, the gossip of the highway; some of it, the instinct of passing events; some of it, *knowledge*. And I cannot let you go down to the Valley without saying what is in my mind. How far it is either gossip, or instinct, or knowledge you—you observe I do not say "you alone"—know. Now, I do *not* regard you as the unadulterated human monstrosity you are depicted by the Verdict and the Judgment. That your wife, Cora—poor, unhappy creature—met her death by unnatural means is, I fear, too true. That those dismembered remains were part of her body, I am afraid is also the fact. But was it *your* hand which did the deed, and was it your hand *alone* which sought to destroy all traces of the tragedy? You see, I use the word "tragedy." It *was* a tragedy, wasn't it? And you were sorely tried, weren't you? *De mortuis nil nisi bonum!* Yes, yes—we won't; but *what about the living?* Is there no one in the world who can tell us aught? I decline to believe that alone you did it. I decline to believe that day after day, and night after night, you worked, unaided, at the ghastly task of dissection, dismemberment and destruction. And, above all, I decline to believe that there is not an explanation of the tragedy itself, as yet untold. You see, I know much of your life—your "home life" I was going to say; but it hadn't been that for several years, had it? There were stormy scenes and angry altercations—and you were not always, or originally, the cause of them. That, at least, it is due to you to say. And more than once she had threatened to poison herself, and more than once you had said you wished she would. *Did she?* Or did someone else administer the fatal drug? And, in your fright, and horror, did you then lose your mental balance?

You must remember it. Tell me, by what superhuman strength was the body of a heavy woman carried down below? Did you alone do that, and, in addition, dig the floor, remove the clay, cover up, rebrick and make good—you, a little, half-blind, elderly, weak and timid man? And, including the butchery, all in twenty-four hours! I am assuming, you see, that no one else was concerned in the affair, and that when anyone called at your house after the period I have mentioned all was peaceful and orderly. Did you alone get rid of the head, the legs, the arms; powder up the bones, the skull? And all in twenty-four hours! And tell me this: Hadn't your wife £200 in a certain Savings Bank? Wasn't the money drawn out immediately after the tragedy? If so, *by whom? Who signed the receipts in her name?*

It is a great mystery. Won't you unravel it? Or may it be that, black as you are painted, you will go to the scaffold with lips sealed in loyalty? Verily, Truth is stranger than fiction!   JOHN BULL.

This communication was duly brought to Crippen's notice, and on Monday last its contents were discussed by him in his final interview with Mr. Arthur Newton, his solicitor.

CRIPPEN'S REPLY.

At the end of the interview, this reply was sent to us through Mr. Newton :—

Pentonville Prison,
Monday, Nov. 21st, 1910.

To the Editor of JOHN BULL.

DEAR SIR,—I am extremely grateful to you for the interest you have taken in me, and I am much touched by some of the passages in your letter. I am not, however, in a position to-day to say much more.

As to making any statement which could implicate anybody else in this terrible business, that is altogether out of the question. I have only just heard the Home Secretary's decision, and to-morrow I am expecting to see an old friend—to whom I may possibly say more than I can now.

I wish, however, to say most emphatically that under no circumstances shall I say anything which would bring trouble to others. Mr. Newton has not only been my solicitor, but, especially during these past few dreadful weeks, has been a sincere friend to me in my trouble. He has my fullest confidence, and I am leaving all my affairs in his hands.

If when it is all over, he cares to tell you more than I can say to-day, I am sure you will treat the matter in the same broad and sympathetic spirit in which you have written me—and that in any case you will not forget poor Miss Le Neve if in any way you can be of assistance to her.

Again thanking you for your kindly expressions,

H. H. CRIPPEN.

[*Next week we hope to be in a position to give the True Story of the Crime—which has never yet been told.*]

SPECIAL NOTICE.

This Week's "Mrs. Bull" contains an Open Letter to

MISS LE NEVE,

and Next Week's "Mrs. Bull" will contain

MISS LE NEVE'S REPLY,

which has already been received.

878   JOHN BULL   DECEMBER 3RD, 1910.

THE CRIPPEN CASE.

THE TRUTH AT LAST — WHO WAS THE CONFEDERATE? — THE ALLEGED "CONFESSION." MORE REMARKABLE LETTERS.

On the eve of Crippen's execution, the new paper, *The Evening Times*, startled the world with the announcement that he had made a full confession, and on the following day, even as the wretched man was walking to the scaffold, our contemporary was busy turning out thousands of copies containing what purported to be the full and true story of the tragedy. Upon examination, we found what professed to be a summary of a statement alleged to have been made by Crippen " to an old friend "—"when all hope of life had passed." Now let us say at once that we know those who are responsible for *The Evening Times* well enough to be satisfied that they would never have been party to anything in any way dishonourable to the newspaper profession. Nor will we tolerate the idea that British journalism is so depraved that any organ of the Press would lend itself to catch-penny sensationalism in regard to so ghastly a subject. We are certain that the paper acted in perfect good faith—although, as we shall show, a little enquiry would have revealed that there was a missing link somewhere. The statement is said to have been made to " an old friend," and made only " when all hope of life had passed." Now, the only " old friend " whom Crippen saw after all hope had passed was Miss Le Neve—and we know it was not made to her ! And the only other person he saw at all was Mr. Arthur Newton, his solicitor, who, in answer to our special enquiry, wrote us on November 23rd, as follows :—

> In reply to your enquiry, I beg to say that the alleged confession appearing in to-day's *Evening Times* is unauthorised as far as I am concerned ; and that Dr. Crippen made no confession to me.

We thus get rid of the only persons whom the condemned man saw after his conviction. But that is not all. *He was never seen, except in the presence of three warders ;* and we have the official statement from Pentonville that nobody there knew anything of a Confession.

Our contemporary will, therefore, see that the individual, whoever he was, who brought the alleged Confession and represented that it was a statement *made to him* " after all hope of life had passed," was practising deception, and, if receiving payment for the story, obtaining money by false pretences. It will further see that it very greatly overstepped the mark when saying that it " possessed unimpeachable authority " for the genuineness of the statement. The " old friend " fiction we shall deal with later.

THE ORIGIN OF THE STATEMENT.

Having said so much, however, it is but fair that we should say something else. The statements contained in the alleged " Confession " *are, in the main, true.* As we shall show, there are a few gaps to be filled ; but, speaking generally, *The Evening Times* did obtain the gist of a statement made by Crippen—*although made*

some time before, and not after, his conviction—and we congratulate the Editor upon his enterprise. Crippen *did* admit " being a party "—we ask our readers to bear these words in mind—to his wife's death ; and he did admit " being a party " to the mutilation, destruction and concealment of her remains. When, and to whom, these admissions were made we are fully aware. How we come to be so is our business ; but we make the assertion with a full sense of responsibility —and, if any reader doubts our word, we hope he will be a reader no longer. If any contemporary doubts us, then it must have a poor opinion, indeed, of the honour of the calling to which it belongs.

AN IMPUDENT DISCLAIMER.

And here let us pause for a moment to notice a most impudent disclaimer by Miss Le Neve's solicitors— her new solicitors—of the genuineness of the reply from Crippen (which we published last week) to our recent Open Letter. Here is the letter which they addressed to the *Daily Chronicle* and other journals :—

> TO THE EDITOR OF THE *Daily Chronicle.*
>
> SIR,—May we ask you if you will be good enough in the interests of our client, Miss Ethel Le Neve who is the sole beneficiary and executrix under the will of the late Dr. H. H. Crippen, to permit us to state in your columns that we have information that the letter printed in JOHN BULL, of the 26th inst.; purporting to have been signed by Dr. Crippen, and dated " Pentonville Prison, Monday, Nov. 21st," was not written or signed by him ?
>
> No such letter was sent out of the prison.
>
> We shall also be obliged if you will permit us to state most emphatically that Dr. Crippen made no confession.
>
> Your obedient servants.,
> HOPWOOD AND SONS.
> 13, South Square, Gray's Inn, W.C.

We are considering the advisability of taking serious steps against certain papers which, without troubling to make any enquiry, gave publicity to a specious libel.

Messrs. Hopwood and Sons are aware, or should be aware, of the manner and the circumstances in which Crippen's reply was conveyed to us. Perhaps they will also challenge the genuineness of the letter from Miss Le Neve which appears in this week's *Mrs. Bull.* After all, Miss Le Neve is now their client, and they have some right, therefore, to speak for her. Besides, there is the additional advantage that Miss Le Neve is still here.

The following letter from Messrs. Arthur Newton and Co. disposes of the matter:—

> TO THE EDITOR OF THE *Daily Chronicle.*
>
> SIR,—Our attention has been called to the letter from Messrs. Hopwood and Sons, appearing in your issue of Saturday. With reference to the answer

from Doctor Crippen to the "Open Letter" recently published in JOHN BULL—which answer appeared in last week's issue of that journal—we beg to say that the same was forwarded through us, after our Mr. Arthur Newton had read the "Open Letter" to Doctor Crippen. On the same day we had an interview with Miss Le Neve, who also handed us a letter written by herself, and addressed to the editor of *Mrs. Bull*, in answer to an "Open Letter" to her which had appeared in that journal. This answer we also handed to the editor.—Yours faithfully,

ARTHUR NEWTON AND CO.
23, Great Marlborough Street, Regent Street,
London, W., November 26th.

THE CRIME.

Mrs. Crippen was poisoned by hyoscin, and Crippen admitted being concerned in the affair. Her body, that of a heavy woman, was then carried down to the coal cellar and was gradually disposed of—partly by means of burning most of the flesh and the small bones; partly by sending the large bones away from the house, and partly by burying the remainder of the flesh under the cellar floor. The day Inspector Dew first visited the house, Crippen stood on the loose slab of stone in the cellar whilst talking to him. So far, the statements published in *The Evening Times* are substantially correct. But now come one or two points which require clearing up. We must not, of course, accept Crippen's sworn statement that Miss Le Neve came to Hilldrop Crescent on the day of what we may now call the murder. She tells us in her letter in this week's *Mrs. Bull* that she was not there for "some days" after the "disappearance," but she adds that when she got there, although frequently in the kitchen and the cellar, she never saw anything unusual, and that Crippen "was calm and quiet, just as usual." We have, therefore, to ask ourselves whether it was possible for Crippen, quite a small and weak man, to have done all the ghastly work, alone and unaided, in a few days—carrying a heavy body down to the cellar, dissecting it, burning the small bones and some of the flesh; getting rid of the others; removing part of the brick floor of the cellar, burying some of the body, and making good the floor. No disorder in the house, no smell, no excitement! The thing is ridiculous. Then, who was the confederate? We tried to get Crippen to say, and listen to this guarded reply:—

Under no circumstances shall I say anything which would bring trouble to others.

"Under no circumstances SHALL I say anything"—a significant phrase, surely! Who, then, was the confederate?

A CLUE.

There is only one clue we can suggest. We have good reason to believe that immediately after Mrs. Crippen's death a sum of money—£200—which stood in the name of the dead woman, in a certain Savings Bank, *was drawn out upon what purported to be her signature.*

In our Open Letters to both Crippen and Miss Le Neve we asked for information upon this point—but none has been forthcoming. Who knows but that here may be the clue to the mystery?

THAT "OLD FRIEND."

Now a word about that "old friend" from whom *The Evening Times* is supposed to have got its statement. That Crippen was expecting to see such a person is clear from his message to us in reply to our letter—"To-morrow"—that was Tuesday, the date upon which *The Evening Times* announced the "Confession"—"I am expecting to see an old friend." But he saw no one except Miss Le Neve, and this is what she wrote after the interview—we have the original letter before us:—

I do, indeed, pray that God will prove his innocence of the crime for which he was convicted, and which do not, neither do I consider he knew anything about. May God help us both at this hour, and bring us together in eternity, is the wish of the woman who loves him, and who would, had she been able to, clear his name before the end. God, however, wills it that we should separate, but I pray that He will assist my efforts in proving to the world his innocence, so that I can go to him with my duty finished.

CRIPPEN'S REMARKABLE PHRASE.

But we have before us also a letter from Crippen, written the day before his execution. It refers to an alteration he had made in his will, and there occurs this remarkable phrase. He is speaking of a will he made in Brixton Prison, when awaiting trial, and he says:—

There was at that time a question, of course, whether or not Ethel would be free. Since then, however, the situation has been changed, Ethel being free.

Despite his knowledge of her absolute innocence, Crippen was evidently doubtful as to whether Miss Le Neve would be justly treated. That, of course, is the only proper construction to place upon the phrase.

DEVOTION TO MISS LE NEVE.

Indeed, the one outstanding feature in the whole of this sordid story is Crippen's devotion to this young woman. In the same letter from which we have quoted occur these passages:—

I have felt it was her due to show the world how entirely I trusted her. . . . I want the public to know I recognise her right to take her place as the woman who has been a true and faithful wife to me for four years, giving me the only true happiness I have ever had, and devoting the best of her life to me . . . my beloved wife.

TO SUM UP.

To sum up, Crippen was party to the murder of his wife. He had a confederate. Somebody used Mrs. Crippen's name, immediately after her death, for the purpose of withdrawing a sum of money from a bank. And somebody took, or sent, some of the bones away from the house. Crippen died in loyalty to that somebody—whoever he or she was. *But something more may yet come to light.* Murder will out.

THE CRIPPEN MYSTERY.

This Week's MRS. BULL contains Miss Le Neve's reply to the Open Letter to her, which recently appeared in that Journal. Everybody interested in the elucidation of the Crippen mystery should

216   MRS. BULL.   DECEMBER 3RD, 1910.

THE CRIPPEN CASE.

MISS LE NEVE REPLIES TO OUR LETTER, AND EXPRESSES HER CONFIDENCE IN CRIPPEN'S INNOCENCE.

Readers will remember that last week the following letter appeared in this journal :—

MY DEAR SISTER,—I have no doubt that you have seen the letter to Dr. Crippen in last week's *John Bull*. It is an appeal, you know, to him to tell us all he could about that terrible tragedy. John feels certain—and I am inclined to agree with him—that the true story has not been told. He does not doubt—as I do not—that poor Belle Elmore met her death by unnatural means, and that those ghastly remains discovered in the cellar at Hilldrop Crescent were part of her mutilated and dismembered body. But he has learnt things about her life and her relations with her husband, which, to put it mildly, make him wonder.

Well, Ethel, there is not much time left, if anything is to be said or done before it is too late. This is Tuesday, and to-morrow—well, you know.

Now what *I* am wondering is whether, perhaps, *you* could help us in any way. Of course, I know, if the poor woman was murdered—as the jury have declared—you can tell us nothing about it. That is settled. You were charged with having been an accessory after the fact ; you pleaded " Not Guilty," and, without another word passing your lips, the jury acquitted you ; and we are all bound to not only accept, but also to respect, that verdict. I do both. But, that said, may not it be that you may be able to throw some light on the mystery, or, even now, at the eleventh hour, to persuade Crippen to do so ? You knew him so well, and you lived in the house so long. Besides, you are said to have been there (mark you, I don't say you *were*) on February 2nd—before Mrs. Crippen had been dead twenty-four hours. Were you ? If so, can you recall anything special which occurred about that time ? Was Crippen much disturbed ; was he frequently alone, down in the kitchen, or the cellar ; did you notice any strange smell—hear any strange noises ? Did you happen to see Mrs. Crippen about that time—have tea with her, perhaps ? Anything said about her unhappy relations with her husband, or money matters, or professional prospects ? Anything said about " wishing she were out of it all," or anything like that ? No " scene," I suppose—no quarrel ? Try and remember. You see, she *might* have committed suicide, and Crippen, in his fright—and fearing the look of things—might have decided to destroy all trace of the remains. But it must have taken a long time—mustn't it ? And a lot of parcels must have left the house—mustn't they ? Can't recall anything, I suppose, of that kind ? Never noticed, in going over the linen, half a pair of pyjamas missing ? Or a loose stone in the floor of the cellar—when getting the coals ? Never saw any strange person in the house about that time ? And did you ever hear anything about a sum of £200 which was deposited in a certain savings bank, and was *drawn out, on somebody's signature, within a few days of Belle Elmore's disappearance ?*

You see, it's all so strange, and, for aught we know, Crippen may not be quite so guilty as he is painted. Perhaps, having told stupid and clumsy stories at the outset, he thought it too late to go back and admit any knowledge of the facts. I need not point out to you that if it were a case of suicide, and if anyone could have corroborated that version, no jury could have convicted. But, of course, that defence would have involved others—and who knows but that, sitting in his silent cell and waiting for the dread morning to arrive, Crippen may not, even now, be engaged in a stern struggle between self-preservation, on the one hand, and, on the other, that strange conception of personal loyalty which has always baffled the students of criminology ?

I do wish you could help us. As things at present stand, Crippen goes to the gallows to-morrow morning ; and I am not comfortable in my mind about it. I am not what is called a very " religious " woman, but the idea of being party to sending a fellow-creature—by a violent death—headlong to eternity, in any case appals me ; and in common with many another woman, I shall not rest peacefully upon my pillow to-morrow night if Dr. Crippen—your lover—goes to his doom without at least *one* voice being raised on his behalf.   MARY BULL.

MISS LE NEVE'S REPLY.
November 22nd, 1910.

DEAR MRS. BULL,

I have read your Open Letter. *I* cannot help you in any way, as I have always said I can throw no light on the mystery. I did not go to Hilldrop Crescent until some days after Mrs. Crippen's disappearance. Dr. Crippen was calm and quiet, just as usual. There was nothing about the house to attract any suspicion whatever. I was often in the kitchen and cellar, and everything was in order. I shall never believe as long as I live that my dear friend, Dr. Crippen, with his amiable, sweet nature, had anything to do with the terrible crime of which he has been convicted ; and his last words to me, even now, when he knows all hope is gone, are to declare his innocence. 20,000 people have signed the Petition for his reprieve ; if these voices are not sufficient what can my poor voice do to save him ?—Yours truly,

E. C. LE NEVE.

This letter will be read with interest. Containing, as it does, Miss Le Neve's explicit declaration that she was not at Hilldrop Crescent till " some days " after Mrs. Crippen's disappearance, and that when she got there she found everything in perfect order, and Crippen " calm and quiet, just as usual," coupled with the statement that she was " often in the kitchen and cellar," and that there " was nothing about the house to attract any suspicion whatever "—surely the mystery deepens ; and everybody will be looking eagerly forward to JOHN BULL's article this week, in which we are promised " the truth at last."

CRIPPEN'S LETTER TO "JOHN BULL."

It may be of interest to here also give a copy of the letter addressed by Crippen to *John Bull*, in reply to the one which recently appeared in that journal :—

Pentonville Prison,
Monday, Nov. 21st, 1910.

DEAR SIR,—I am extremely grateful to you for the interest you have taken in me, and I am much touched by some of the passages in your letter. I am not, however, in a position to-day to say much more.

As to making any statement which will implicate anybody else in this terrible business, that is altogether out of the question. I have only just heard the Home Secretary's decision, and to-morrow I am expecting to see an old friend—to whom I may possibly say more than I can now.

I wish, however, to say most emphatically that under no circumstances shall I say anything which would bring trouble to others. Mr. Newton has not only been my solicitor, but, especially during these past few dreadful weeks, has been a sincere friend to me in my trouble. He has my fullest confidence, and I am leaving all my affairs in his hands.

If, when it is all over, he cares to tell you more than I can say to-day, I am sure you will treat the matter in the same broad and sympathetic spirit in which you have written me—and that in any case you will not forget poor Miss Le Neve if in any way you can be of assistance to her.

Again thanking you for your kindly expressions,

H. H. CRIPPEN.

At the time of going to press, the "EVENING TIMES" is publishing what purports to be a "confession." As a matter of fact, JOHN BULL—and JOHN BULL only—has the story.

THE NEW YORK TIMES, THURSDAY, NOVEMBER 24, 1910.

Conviction of Crippen.

To the Editor of The New York Times:

I have read both the New York and the London accounts of the Crippen case, being interested through the fact that I lived for many years within a few minutes' walk from the house where the crime was committed and also passed the house in July, just after Crippen had disappeared.

I am at a total loss to understand why many people on this side of the Atlantic can be so biased at English court methods. Is it because of the contrast to American methods?

One paper in Chicago published an article to the effect that Crippen could not have chosen a worse country than England in which to commit murder. It is not difficult to read between the lines the real meaning of this remark. If I may give my opinion, allow me to say that if I ever contemplated committing a serious crime I would choose America in preference to England in which to carry out the deed, solely for the fact that the numerous courts of appeal, combined with peculiar methods of construing Blackstone and interpretations of the meaning of the law, would give me a favorable chance of cheating justice and ultimately gaining my freedom.

New York, Nov. 22, 1910.   ELDDEW.

"THE BODY OF THE CRIME."

Dr. HARVEY HAWLEY CRIPPEN, who was hanged yesterday in an English prison for the willful murder of his wife, would have been alive to-day and a free man had his crime been committed in this State. According to the New York statute law the prosecution would have had to establish by direct proof the identity of the human remains found under quicklime bricked up in CRIPPEN's cellar.

Indirectly the corpus delicti, or body of the crime, was sufficiently proved in the English trial. A scar was found remarkably like one known to be borne by BELLE ELMORE CRIPPEN. Clothing, dyed hair, and other articles similar to those possessed by the doctor's wife were discovered in the cellar, while in the remains were traces of a rare poison such as CRIPPEN had purchased shortly before she disappeared. The sex of the body was not established; the evidence was wholly circumstantial. But, according to the common law of England, where such agents as quicklime are used to destroy the evidence of murder, the rule of the corpus delicti may not prevail.

The leading American case is that of EDWARD H. RULOFF. In 1856, before the present New York statute was enacted, RULOFF was convicted by a jury of the murder of his child, who, together with his wife, had disappeared on the day before RULOFF was seen to cart off a box in his wagon near the shores of a lake in Tompkins County. A heavy weight disappeared from his premises on the same day. RULOFF then ran away. As the wife and child were never seen afterward, it seemed clear to the prosecution and to the jury that the accused had sunk their bodies in the lake. But the Court of Appeals in 1858 reversed the conviction on the ground of lack of direct evidence. RULOFF was later convicted and hanged for a subsequent murder.

This reversal was had at common law. Why, after such a demonstration of its restraining power a later statute should have been passed making the rule of the corpus delicti inflexible is a matter of marvel. Should not the statute be repealed?

Clarkson Rose writes:

39 Hilldrop Crescent continued an association with the variety theatre, because a comedian named Sandy McNab occupied it, and he, too, became notorious; and later still part of the premises were used as a theatre- and music-hall wardrobe, with which I was partly associated, and I cannot say that I ever felt any strange or eerie sensation when I went there with other artists for meetings and fittings.

AFTERWORDS

"PARKFIELD".
THE HEATH.
Cheshire. RUNCORN.
5th. Jany. 1925

Sir William Willcox, K.C.I.E.,
St. Mary's Hospital, W.2.

Dear Sir

As I am very interested in Forensic Chemistry and its allied Sciences, I am venturing to ask if you would be so good as to explain a point, arising in your lecture, which I have difficulty in understanding: Viz. the action of quicklime on the human body after death.

You state that the quicklime in which Crippen buried his wife's viscera, acted as a preservative, without which the hyoscine might never have been isolated. Further Lucas in his "Forensic Chemistry" describes some experiments made with dead pigeons which go to show that quick lime undoubtedly preserves animal matter after death.

I should be most grateful if you would be good enough

to explain the true nature of the chemical action of the lime upon the body, and I sincerely trust that you will pardon what may, perhaps, appear to be presumption on my part in approaching you thus.

I am, dear Sir,

Yours faithfully,

H.G. Stevenson Coppin

9th January 1925.

Dear Sir,

With reference to your enquiry about the action of quicklime. This, as you know, rapidly becomes hydrated and the calcium hydrate, owing to its alkalinity, is a fairly efficient antiseptic. Also the calcium hydrate combines with the fat of viscera forming a calcium soap called adipocera which forms a protecting coating round viscera.

For those two reasons quicklime acts as a preservative if viscera are buried in it.

I am,

Yours very truly,

H.G. Stevenson Coppin Esq.
Parkfield,
The Heath, Runcorn.
Cheshire.

Walter Dew retired from the police force on 5 November 1910, the day after Crippen's appeal was rejected. He could well afford to take early retirement: he had won, or could win, libel actions against nine newspapers for misquoting him "to the detriment of his professional reputation"; most of the actions were settled out of court for undisclosed sums, but some idea of how much Dew received can be gained from the fact that he won £400 damages, plus costs, from the *Daily Chronicle*. (There are no figures for the internal purchasing power of the pound before 1914. The 1914 pound was worth approximately twenty-nine times more than the present-day pound; to put it another way, today's pound is worth about 3.4 pence compared with the 1914 pound.)

In 1911, Mr Dew paid 200 guineas cash for a house in Perivale Lane, Greenford, West London (next to Ealing Golf Club); he called the house "The Nook".

By 1934, he had moved from "The Nook" to "The Wee Hoose" in the south-coast resort of Worthing.

"The Wee Hoose,"
16 Beaumont Road,
Worthing.

10th July, 1934.

To
The Editor,
"The Daily Mail",
Northcliffe House,
London, E.C.

Dear Sir,

Re "What a Big Crime Costs the Nation".

I was interested to read the above mentioned article in to-days "Daily Mail".

I was more than interested, and indeed staggered, at the statement therein as follows:-

"Dr. Crippin, the murderer of Belle Elmore, his actress wife made a dash for Canada with a woman companion. Before the first wireless used in crime, reached England - it revealed the whereabouts of Crippen - something like £10,000 had been spent in the search for him."

As the Officer in charge of the inquiries, and the one who chased and captured him in Canada, I should know something about the expenses incurred up to the time stated.   I am puzzled indeed to know how £10,000 was spent ?

Not one extra police officer was recruited and the pay of those engaged would still have gone on, whether Crippen had committed a crime or not, so it cannot be said that that was an extra charge on the Nation, and I doubt if my own expenses

-2-

for cab fares up to the time the wireless was received, exceeded £2, and the extra costs, whilst I was making enquiries, as a Chief Inspector, for food allowance, would be 3/- per day, always supposing I could not reach home for a meal for a continuous period of nine hours, other officers of less rank would be paid in proportion.

Of course there was the printing of the Reward bills and other expenses, such as medical men, etc., and I should have thought I was exaggerating if I had suggested that up to the time of the wireless being received the cost would not have exceeded £500.

Maybe, Mr. Hugh Brady has some information as to the expenses incurred which I am ignorant of, but oh ! £10,000 extra cost to the Nation before that famous wireless was received and that in 1910, too !

I really should be glad to be enlightened, and doubtless, so would the taxpayers.

I am, Sir,

Your obedient Servant,

Ex Chief Inspector,
C.I. Dept.,
New Scotland Yard.

A cutting from the *Worthing Gazette* of 10 August 1938, pasted into Dew's scrapbook:

ex-Inspector Dew.

WHEN CRIPPEN WAS ARRESTED.

28 YEARS AGO THIS WEEK.

EX-SCOTLAND YARD INSPECTOR RECALLS EXCITING CHASE.

Twenty-eight years ago this week, perspiring in the heat of a Canadian summer, was a man who had just effected the most sensational criminal capture of the century.

He was Chief-Inspector Walter Dew, of Scotland Yard, who is now living in retirement at Worthing—at The Wee Hoose, 10, Beaumont-road,—and in talking this week to a *Worthing Gazette* representative Mr. Dew let his mind go back to that exciting summer of 1910 when he raced to Quebec to intercept Dr. Hawley Harvey Crippen, the murderer of his wife, Belle Elmore, before he could make his escape on Canadian soil.

"Twenty-eight years ago to-day," said Mr. Dew, " Crippen was already safe inside the gaol on the Heights of Abraham. As for myself, I was simply sweltering in the hot and humid atmosphere of the city.

" Much of my time was spent evading reporters and cameramen—who knew all about my arrival in spite of our efforts to keep it secret, and who frequently became personal when I did not give them a statement—visiting Crippen in gaol (he was continually asking for new books to read), and making arrangements for the return to England.

On Sunday, July 31st, Inspector Dew, disguised as a pilot'-officer, went on board the "Montrose' from a pilot vessel off Father Point, and, immediately recognising the murderer, made the arrest.

"Old Crippen took it quite well," he said. " He always was a bit of a philosopher, though he could not have helped being astounded to see me on board the boat. . . . He was quite a likeable chap in his way."

Then followed the days of waiting while the formalities were gone into, until finally, on August 20th, the " Megantic " left Quebec with captor and captives on board, bound for the Old Bailey and the final episodes in the drama which is fully described by Inspector Dew in his recent book, "I Caught Crippen."

IN MEMORY OF THE VICTIM.

Worthing has another link with the Crippen case in addition to Mr. Dew's residence here.

The memorial stone which was placed over the remains of Mrs. Crippen—professionally known as Belle Elmore—in St. Pancras Cemetery was executed and erected by the late Councillor Francis Tate, the father of Mr. Francis Tate who now carries on the monumental mason's works in North-street.

It took the form of a headstone in Greek statuary marble, with a heavily moulded hood and a deeply sunk panel from which a Latin cross and bases stood out in high relief; and upon this was the simple inscription:

" In Memoriam, Cora Crippen (Belle Elmore), who passed away 1st Feb., 1910. Rest in peace."

Walter Dew died, aged eighty-four, on 16 December 1947.

Obituary 29 Nov 1965

Capt. Kendall sent 'Crippen aboard' signal

CAPT. HENRY GEORGE KENDALL, who died yesterday in a London nursing home aged 91, was primarily responsible for the arrest in Canadian waters in 1910 of Dr. Crippen.

He used the then novel wireless to inform Scotland Yard of his suspicions.

Before he left Antwerp in his ship, the Canadian Pacific liner Montrose, he had read of the hunt for Dr. Hawley Harvey Crippen, whose wife's remains had been found buried in the cellar of their home in Hilldrop Crescent, Camden Town.

Crippen and his companion, Miss Ethel Le Neve, had disappeared.

Soon after the voyage began Capt. Kendall detected something unusual about two of the passengers, a Mr. Robinson and his "son." His suspicions of their true identity increased to the point when he sent his wireless message to Scotland Yard: "Crippen and Miss Le Neve are in the Montrose."

Couple arrested

As sparks crackled from the ship's radio installation Crippen was said to have commented: "What a wonderful invention radio is." But for the first time radio had trapped a murderer.

Chief Insp. Dew, of Scotland Yard, crossed to Canada in a faster vessel, boarded the Montrose at Father Point, near the mouth of the St. Lawrence, and arrested the couple.

Capt. H. G. Kendall

Crippen was hanged at Pentonville. Miss Le Neve, accused as an accomplice, was acquitted.

In 1939 Capt. Kendall, born in Chelsea, retired from his post as marine superintendent for the Canadian Pacific at Surrey Commercial Docks. His wife died in 1940. He leaves two sons and a daughter.

Accounts and Transmutations

There are three hardback books devoted to the case: *Trial of Hawley Harley Crippen*, edited by Filson Young, in the "Notable British Trials" series (William Hodge & Co. Ltd., Edinburgh, 1919); *Crippen: The Mild Murderer* by Tom Cullen (The Bodley Head, London, 1977) and – not worth searching for – *Doctor Crippen* by Max Constantine-Quinn (Duckworth, London, 1935).

The best of the paperback monographs is *Doctor Crippen* by Michael Gilbert (Odhams Press Ltd., London, 1953).

Ethel Le Neve: Her Life Story, "Told by Herself", first printed in *Lloyd's Weekly News* of 6 and 13 November 1910, was soon afterwards published as a threepenny paperback by John Long Ltd., London; a year or so later, Jesse Pemberton, proprietor of the Daisy Bank Printing & Publishing Co., Gorton, Manchester, brought out an edition of the Life Story, without having asked anyone for permission to do so, and then produced *Full Account of the Crippen Horror*. (See "The Publications of Jesse Pemberton" by Jonathan Goodman: *Antiquarian Book Monthly Review*, Oxford, January 1985.)

At the end of *Murder: Plain and Fanciful* (Sheridan House, New York, 1948), the editor, James Sandoe, presents a "Criminal Clef: Tales and Plays Based on Real Crimes", which includes the following entries:

BLACKWELL, DONALD (and THEODORE ST JOHN). *The Distant Shore* (1935). This play owes a good deal to the Crippen case according to Bushnell Dimond, a belief shared by Burns Mantle in his synopsis of the play (*Best Plays* of 1934-1935).

MEADOWS, CATHERINE. *Dr Moon* (English title: *Henbane*) Earle F. Walbridge (*Literary Characters Drawn From Life*, New York, 1936) calls this novel "a sympathetic statement . . . of the murder of his wife (who seemed to ask for it) by Dr Hawley Harvey Crippen."

VAN DRUTEN, JOHN. "The Cat's Eye" (in the *Atlantic Monthly*, March 1945). Anthony Boucher calls this "Crippenesque".

To the above may be added two novels by Ernest Raymond, *We, the Condemned* (Cassell, London, 1935) and *A Chorus Ending* (Cassell, London, 1951), and Ursula Bloom's *The Girl Who Loved Crippen* (Hutchinson, London, 1954). Also a three-act play, *They Fly by Twilight* by Paul Dornhorst, first produced at the People's Palace, London, on 7 June 1937, and then at the Q Theatre, Kew, Surrey, on 19 September 1938 (published in 1939), in *Five Plays of Our Time* edited by Sydney Box, and separately in 1940, in both instances by Thomas Nelson, London); *Dearly Beloved Wife* by Jeanne De Casalis, presented by the London Playgoers' Club at the Vaudeville Theatre, in the Strand, on 30 October 1938 (the

small part of "Mitchell" was played by a young actor named Trevor Howard); *Belle, or The Ballad of Dr Crippen,* "a music-hall musical" by Monty Norman and Wolf Mankowitz, which ran for six weeks from 4 May 1961 at the Strand Theatre. In the last-mentioned entertainment, Crippen described in the introductory notes as "one of the great lovers of forensic history" — was depicted by George Benson. Acting as a form of chorus, a character named Lasher, a music-hall comedian and one of Belle's beaux, sang "The Ballad of Doctor Crippen" as a link between scenes. The following are extracts:

> Here's a little story,
> A touching tale of woe:
> Happened here in London
> 'Bout fifty years ago.
> A little Yankee doctor
> Created quite a din,
> All because he gave his
> Dear wife a Mickey-Finn.
> Funny little dentist,
> Crippen was his name,
> Pulled his patients' teeth out
> With very little pain.
> In his little surgery
> He was so up-to-date —
> Ultra-modern equipment
> To do you while you wait.
> Ethel was his sweetheart,
> His secretary and nurse;
> He loved her by appointment
> But flies got in the ointment
> When that handsome Lasher
> Had had enough of Belle.

> Funny little fellow,
> Crippen was his name.
> Might not get to Canada —
> Let's hope so just the same.

> Poor old Doctor Crippen,
> The net is closing in;
> Someone on the Montrose
> Has set the police on him.

> Funny little fellow,
> Ethel by his side,
> There in the Old Bailey
> For murder they were tried

> When the trial was over,
> The jury, sad to tell,
> Found old Crippen guilty
> Of killing poor old Belle.

> Then one early morning
> The hangman took his toll;
> May the Lord have mercy
> On poor old Crippen's soul.

> Funny little fellow,
> Crippen was his name;
> See him for a sixpence
> In the Hall of Fame.

As for films, *The Suspect* (1944) had Charles Laughton as a London shopkeeper who murders his wife, partly because of her spiteful nature, partly because he is in love with a younger woman (played by Ella Raines), and in *Doctor Crippen* (1962), Donald Pleasance was the Doctor, Coral Browne played Belle, Samantha Eggar appeared as Ethel, Donald Wolfit was Richard Muir, and John Arnatt portrayed Inspector Dew.

ETHEL LE NEVE

HER LIFE STORY

WITH THE TRUE ACCOUNT OF THEIR FLIGHT
AND HER FRIENDSHIP FOR

DR. CRIPPEN

ALSO STARTLING PARTICULARS OF HER LIFE
AT HILLDROP CRESCENT

TOLD BY HERSELF

Published by

THE DAISY BANK PRINTING & PUBLISHING CO.,
WELLINGTON STREET, GORTON, MANCHESTER.
Telephone No. 696 Openshaw.

Roland Young as Dr. Crippen in "The Distant Shore"

The Times, 23 November

OUTWARD-BOUND STEAMERS

| New York . . | . . Cunard | Liverp'l, | Nov. 26 |
| Do. (S.S. Majestic) White Star | | . . S'th'ton, | Nov. 23 |

The *Majestic* sailed at noon, three hours after the execution at Pentonville. Ethel Le Neve was on board. Dressed in mourning, a veil hiding her face, she was entered on the passenger-list as "Miss Allen".

She stayed in New York only a day or so, then travelled to Toronto, where – still as "Miss Allen" – she reverted to earning her living as a typist.

Early in 1911, she was granted probate of Crippen's will, valued at £268. An application on her behalf for probate of the estate of Mrs Crippen having been turned down, letters of administration were granted to the victim's sister, Mrs Theresa Hunn.

Ethel returned to England, to London, in 1914, and worked as a typist at Hampton's furniture store in Trafalgar Square. She was using Crippen's middle name, Harvey, as her surname. Stanley Smith, a clerk at Hampton's, shyly courted her, plucked up the courage to propose marriage, and was accepted.

The couple moved into a house at Croydon, on the southern outskirts of the metropolis, and in time were blessed with children, a son and a daughter. Years passed: the children married . . . Stanley died of a heart attack a few days before his seventieth birthday, when he had planned to retire . . . in 1943, Ethel became eligible for an old-age pension from the State. In the summer of 1967, she was taken in to hospital, terminally ill.

Nearly fifty-seven years before, her letters to Crippen – known to her as "Hub" – had, at his request, been buried with him. Ethel's last request – so it is said – was that a locket holding a faded likeness of Crippen be placed close to her heart before her coffin was closed.

Stanley Smith with his and Ethel's son.

Application Number Y12428

	REGISTRATION DISTRICT	Camberwell						
1967. DEATH in the Sub-district of		Dulwich			in the London Borough of Southwark			
Columns:—	1	2	3	4	5	6	7	8	9
No.	When and where died	Name and surname	Sex	Age	Occupation	Cause of death	Signature, description, and residence of informant	When registered	Signature of registrar
314	Ninth August 1967 Dulwich Hospital East Dulwich	Ethel Clara Smith	Female	84 years	of 62 Burford Road Lewisham Widow of Stanley William Smith Builders General Clerk	1(a) Cardiac failure (b) Mitral incompetence Certified by J R Sutton Coulson M.B. B.S.		Tenth August 1967	S M MacDonald Deputy Registrar

AN END

MADAME TUSSAUD'S